2010
Mission Yearbook
for Prayer & Study

*Out of the believer's
heart shall flow rivers
of living water.*

John 7:38

Witherspoon Press • Louisville, Kentucky

PRESBYTERIAN CHURCH (USA)

The Presbyterian Church (U.S.A.)'s *Mission Yearbook for Prayer & Study* is published by Witherspoon Press and produced by members of the Mission Interpretation team, General Assembly Mission Council.

The *2010 Mission Yearbook for Prayer & Study* was prepared by Margaret Hall Boone, senior administrative assistant; Denise Dukes, senior administrative assistant; Elder Billie Healy, editor; Bryce Hudson, Web designer; Elder Carol E. Johnson, designer and formatter; Susan Salsburg, copy editor; Mark Thomson, designer and formatter; and Kathy Wolpert, senior administrative assistant.

Cover

The cover was designed by Elder Carol E. Johnson using images from the 2010 yearbook to illustrate the theme.

Color Insert Section

"Presbyterian Women in Mission: Together We Witness to the Promise—Yesterday, Today, and Tomorrow"
This section was written by Carissa Herold and designed by Stephanie Morris.

Color Insert Section

"The Year 2010: Two Anniversaries in the History of American Protestant Missions"
This section was written by the Rev. Michael Parker and designed by Elder Carol E. Johnson.

 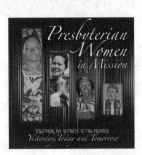

Ordering Information

To order additional copies of the *2010 Mission Yearbook for Prayer & Study*, call Presbyterian Distribution Service at (800) 524-2612.

To reserve your copy of the *2011 Mission Yearbook for Prayer & Study*, please call Presbyterian Distribution Service at (800) 524-2612 or use the bound-in order form. Books will be mailed before October 30, 2010.

Correspondence

Please direct correspondence to:
Editor, *Mission Yearbook for Prayer & Study*
Presbyterian Church (U.S.A.)
100 Witherspoon Street
Louisville, KY 40202–1396
(888) 728-7228, ext. 5689
billie.healy@pcusa.org

Acknowledgments

We are grateful for assistance in the production of this book provided by Nancy Goodhue and the Rev. David Gambrell, as well as the contributions and oversight of the Rev. Jon Brown, director of Mission Interpretation. "An Outline for Daily Prayer" was prepared by the Rev. Teresa Lockhart Stricklen.

Elder Linda B. Valentine is the executive director of the GAMC and Elder Karen Schmidt is deputy executive director of Communications and Funds Development.

Contents

Alphabetical Listing

Alphabetical Listing

Alphabetical Listing

Alphabetical Listing

Minute for Mission Listing

Welcome to the *2010 Mission Yearbook for Prayer & Study*

"My family and I have used the "prayer calendar" since childhood and I am now 92 . . . I love it."

"Without question for me the *Mission Yearbook for Prayer & Study* is the most inspirational, informative, and interesting publication that the PC(USA) puts out. I have read it for some 50 years, and each year it is better."

". . . the ministries that still go on in tiny and large churches, in places I only read about where mission personnel share their insights . . . I find it inspirational. There is the continuum of faithful people, living with their differences but clinging hardily to their Savior in order to be faithful witnesses."

For 117 years, Presbyterians have found the *Mission Yearbook for Prayer & Study* a useful guide to their daily time with God. The stories of mission and ministry flow from the hearts of pastors, mission workers, presbytery staffers, and countless others committed to living out the Gospel.

In every story you'll catch a glimpse of the amazing work that God is doing throughout our troubled world. On every page, you'll find the names of faithful believers dedicated to keeping those streams of living water flowing. Within each prayer, you'll join the cloud of witnesses in a holy conversation with the living Lord.

I remember the morning in 1995 when our mission pastor gave me my first copy. I was overwhelmed by the breadth and reach of Presbyterian mission. Today, I know that what is captured in these pages is just the tip of the proverbial iceberg. God is at work in so many ways in so many places and so many lives—it's more than our finite minds can comprehend.

So enjoy. If this is your first encounter with the *Mission Yearbook*, welcome! If you've used and enjoyed it for years, welcome again. Turn the page. Drink from the living water.

—*Elder Rob Bullock, director of mission communications, General Assembly Mission Council*

Prayer

Gracious God, may we drink each day from the living water of your word. And may that living water flow through us, so that others may find what we have found, and receive your love, your mercy, and your blessing. In your Son's name we pray. Amen.

Information about the *Mission Yearbook*

Brief History

The *Mission Yearbook for Prayer & Study* dates back to 1892 when the Women's Executive Committee for Home Mission, Organization of Presbyterian Women, prepared a Calendar of Prayer to help women's societies pray for missionaries on designated days. Now in its 118th year of continuous publication, the *Mission Yearbook* remains a daily voice for the mission of the Presbyterian Church (U.S.A.).

Abbreviations

On the Lord's Day pages, abbreviations identify where hymn selections can be found—PH: *The Presbyterian Hymnal*; WB: *The Worshipbook*; HB: *The Hymnbook*; PPCS: *The Psalter: Psalms and Canticles for Singing*; PCW: *Psalter for Christian Worship*. In the daily prayer lists, abbreviations are used to identify the areas in which General Assembly staff work—APCU: Association of Presbyterian Colleges and Universities; BOP: Board of Pensions; FDN: Presbyterian Church (U.S.A.) Foundation Group; GAMC: General Assembly Mission Council; OGA: Office of the General Assembly; PAM: Presbyterian Association of Musicians; PILP: Presbyterian Investment and Loan Program; PPC: Presbyterian Publishing Corporation.

Lectionary

The lectionary is from the Presbyterian Church (U.S.A.)'s *Book of Common Worship*. The text for Sundays and festivals is originally from the *Revised Common Lectionary*, prepared by the Consultation on Common Texts. The daily lectionary in the *Book of Common Worship* is taken from the *Book of Common Prayer*, with revisions that were made for inclusion in the *Lutheran Book of Worship*.

Scripture

Unless otherwise noted, Scripture quotations are from the New Revised Standard Version of the Bible. They are copyrighted ©1989 by the Division of Christian Education of the National Council of the Churches of Christ in the U.S.A. and are used with permission.

Country Information

The information provided in the shaded box on pages devoted to international countries was taken from the online version of *The World Factbook*, (https://www.cia.gov/library/publications/the-world-factbook/index.html). The information is accurate as of June 8, 2009. For comparison purposes, information on the United States is provided in the shaded box below.

> UNITED STATES
> **Total area:** 3,794,083 sq. mi. (incl. 50 states and Dist. of Columbia; about three-tenths the size of Africa). **Population:** 307,212,123. **Languages:** English, Spanish, other. **GDP per capita:** $47,000. **Literacy:** 99%. **Religions:** Protestant, Roman Catholic, Mormon, Jewish, Muslim, other. **Life expectancy:** 78 years. **Human Development Index rank:** 15.

Human Development Index Rank

The Human Development Index (HDI), developed by the United Nations Development Programme, is a composite index of achievements in three fundamental human dimensions: life expectancy, educational attainment, and income. The shaded boxes include a ranking by HDI values. The HDI rank for the United States is 15 out of 177. Visit http://hdr.undp.org./en/statistics/ for more information and to see the full list.

Mission Personnel

PC(USA) mission co-workers are fully compensated, full-time international mission service workers appointed to work in partnership with overseas ecumenical partner churches or institutions. To become part of the support community for mission personnel, call K.T. Ockels at (888) 728-7228, ext. 5977. Mission Volunteers International and Mission Volunteers in the U.S.A. may receive a subsistence-living stipend and/or room and board for service of several weeks to two years. Additional benefits are available for volunteers serving internationally for a period greater than one year. Only volunteers serving for a year or longer are listed in the *Mission Yearbook*. Learn more about becoming a part of the church's mission through national or international service by calling (888) 728-7228, ext. 2530.

Making the Most of Your *Mission Yearbook*

As a Guide for Daily Bible Reading

The daily lectionary is printed in the bottom corner of each page. This lectionary provides for reading twice through the New Testament and once through the Old Testament during its two-year cycle. Psalm readings are separated into day and evening psalms by these symbols [☼ ☾]. The morning psalms help us rise daily to the newness of life while the evening psalms call to mind God's grace and our dependence on Christ.

The weekly lectionary is printed in the shaded box on the Lord's Day pages and follows a three-year cycle. From this cycle of readings, many Presbyterians throughout the world decide on the Bible verses that will be read in worship on Sundays. Both lectionaries are listed on Lord's Day pages in the *Mission Yearbook for Prayer & Study*.

To Support the Mission of the Church

Engage in a daily ministry with Presbyterians around the world by using the *Mission Yearbook* as you pray each day. Don't hesitate to let people know you prayed for them. It may be just the encouragement they need!

- Mission personnel and volunteers are listed on or near the page featuring the country or presbytery where they serve.
- Members of presbytery and synod staff are listed on the page featuring their synod or presbytery.
- Leaders of our partner churches and organizations are listed on or near the page featuring the country where they are working.
- General Assembly Mission Council (GAMC) members are listed by presbytery.
- Members of General Assembly staff are listed in alphabetical order.

Contribute financially to God's mission through the church. Individuals can send checks to: PC(USA) Individual Remittance Processing, P.O. Box 643700, Pittsburgh PA 15264-3700. Give online through www.pcusa.org/navigation/giving.htm, or call PresbyTel at (800) 872-3283 for more information.

To Expand Your Mission Promotion Capability

Whether you are traveling and have forgotten your *Mission Yearbook* or want to download inspiring mission stories for minutes for mission, the Sunday bulletin, or your church's Web site, visit www.pcusa.org/missionyearbook/choose-day.htm to find the daily entries!

With Companion Resources

2010 Children's Mission Yearbook for Prayer & Study

Never underestimate the power and energy of a kid plugged into God's love! The *Children's Mission Yearbook for Prayer & Study* is a must-read for every child in your congregation! But order extras because big kids love it too! To order call (800) 524-2612.

Transform Lives in the Name of Christ: Presbyterian Mission Personnel 2009

This resource gives a glimpse of the mission-sending ministry supported by the prayers and gifts of Presbyterians. It provides information on all long-term Presbyterian mission personnel and information on how to be part of their ministry. Visit www.pcusa.org/missionconnections/2009-mission-giving-catalog.pdf or call (888) 728-7228, ext. 5172 to request a copy.

Need More Suggestions?

Visit www.pcusa.org/missionyearbook/instructions.htm to see ideas that have been submitted. Send yours in today to mission.yearbook@pcusa.org. Many of the ideas are available in print form in the *Reader's Guide to the Mission Yearbook and the Children's Mission Yearbook* (PDS 70612-06-425). Free copies are available from PDS at (800) 524-2612.

An Outline for Daily Prayer

Out of the believer's heart shall flow rivers of living water. (John 7:38)

Daily prayer gives us a way of offering ourselves to God each day as a vessel of living water that is renewed through the practice of praise and prayer. Without this renewal, whatever Spirit-water we have in us can become stagnant and stale. Indeed, the purpose of being vessels of living water is to be poured out in service to others, not to keep the living water for our own refreshment. Thus, we pray for others as part of our service, and thereby open ourselves to be used as a vessel of God, a veritable sluice of the Water of Life.

We Call Upon the Lord

O God, you are my God, I seek you;
My soul thirsts for you.
Jesus said, "Let anyone who is thirsty come to me.
And let the one who believes in me drink."
You are the Lord, the giver of life,
Who quenches our thirst with Living Water.

With Praise and Thanksgiving

Prayer of Thanksgiving. Pray a spontaneous prayer of thanksgiving for all the good things God has given you. Count your blessings! Naming the things we take for granted that we're grateful for is a wonderful discipline of praise. You may name such things as "for the breath of my body, for this shelter, for those whom you have placed in our/my life, for those who work to keep our society safe, for those who stayed up last night negotiating peace," etc.

Song of Praise. If you're alone, you may make up your own song of praise to sing throughout the day or just burst into your favorite song of praise. You may want to dance your praise. If you're part of a group, find a hymn or song of praise that just thanks God for being God.

To Listen for the Word

Prayer for Illumination. Living Word, send forth your Holy Spirit to open our ears to the sound of your voice. In Christ Jesus we pray. Amen.

Scripture Reading. Read the lectionary passages for the day, pausing to listen for God speaking to you.

To Pray for the World

Read the story for the day in preparation for prayer. Recall those in the news who are in need of prayer. If you keep a prayer journal, bring it and the prayer list from your church bulletin into this prayer as well.

Holy God, you know our thirst for your way among all people. Help us to pray for the world in which we live, matching our prayers to yours

for the resources of this earth . . .
for the world in which we live . . .
for the church and its ministries . . .
for those who are in special need . . .
and for those situations that weigh upon our hearts. . . .

In all these places, work the wonders of your grace according to your perfect will, that your healing presence may transform creation into what you originally intended for the good of all. This we pray through Christ our Lord who taught us to pray, saying . . .

The Lord's Prayer

To Go Forth to Live Our Prayer

May the Lord bless our going out and coming in from this time forth and forevermore.
Amen.
Drenched in the waters of baptism,
We will live this day in thanks and praise!

The Synod of the Sun

Solar energy is now a part of mission in the Synod of the Sun. With inspiration and start-up assistance from the Synod of Living Waters and its Living Waters for the World mission, Synod of the Sun has launched a mission called Solar Under the Sun.

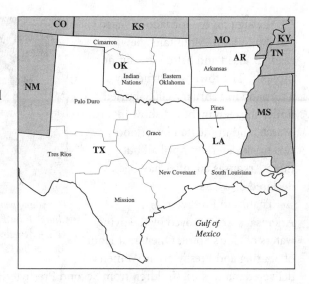

From isolated villages in Haiti to powerless *colonias* near the United States-Mexico border, the eleven presbyteries of this synod will install solar power for specific uses and train residents how to maintain the equipment. The Presbytery of Arkansas, the lead partner in this new venture, houses the "solar school" for volunteers at Ferncliff Camp and Conference Center near Little Rock.

The synod facilitates communication and connects the resources of 175,364 Presbyterians in 873 congregations. In its bounds are sixteen service and educational institutions including Austin Presbyterian Theological Seminary. Presbyterian Mo-Ranch Assembly and Evergreen Presbyterian Ministries have served the region for more than 110 years altogether.

Prayer

Loving God, guide Presbyterians in this synod as they build new mission. Strengthen the growing partnership among your people on both sides of the United States-Mexico border. Bring grace where fear and violence permeate the lives of communities. We seek your guidance in the name of Christ. Amen.

Daily Lectionary
☼ Ps. 98, 148 ☾ Ps. 99, 8
Isa. 62:1–5, 10–12
Rev. 19:11–16; Matt. 1:18–25

Daily Lectionary
☼ Ps. 48, 149 ☾ Ps. 9, 29
1 Kings 19:1–8
Eph. 4:1–16; John 6:1–14

The Presbytery of Arkansas

The sign on the tornado-ravaged building in Mountain View read "Bruised and battered—but not broken!" The town was struck by a tornado in February 2008, buried under thirteen inches of snow in March, and inundated by a flood two weeks later. By April all but three Arkansas counties had been declared disasters.

Two young people from Wynne Presbyterian Church helped their congregation collect $472 for Presbyterian Disaster Assistance "Bucket Bucks."

Lisa Blanton

Thanks to Presbyterians, Arkansans were buoyed by the living waters of God's Spirit. One Great Hour of Sharing and Presbyterian Women delivered mattresses. Children from Second Presbyterian in Little Rock created prayer pillows for children in affected areas. Presbyterians from Fort Smith, Russellville, and Atkins replaced a farmer's fence. Volunteers from the Synod of the Trinity came to serve.

First Presbyterian in Lonoke gave its pastor, the Rev. Emmett Powers, six months' paid leave to coordinate relief efforts. Working out of Ferncliff's Presbyterian Disaster Assistance Center, volunteers built and delivered dozens of storage units for people's rescued possessions.

Even after the natural disasters in Arkansas, volunteers continued to serve New Covenant Presbytery, which had been struck by Hurricane Ike. Arkansas and Grace presbyteries teamed to raise "Bucket Bucks," and volunteers filled more than 2,000 buckets with sponges, scrub brushes, and love.

The Presbytery of Arkansas serves 90 churches, 2 new church developments, 2 fellowships, and 15,197 members. It is also blessed by Lyon College, University of the Ozarks, Vera Lloyd Presbyterian Home and Family Services, and Ferncliff Camp and Conference Center.

Prayer
God of us all, you bear us up amid the storms of life. Thank you for those whose hands and feet you use to bring comfort and healing in your name. Give us glad hearts for service and joy in the serving. In Jesus' name we ask it. Amen.

The Lord's Day

Minute for Mission: Auburn Theological Seminary

"Give your servant therefore an understanding mind . . . , able to discern between good and evil" (1 Kings 3:9).

When speaking of her desire to take part in Auburn's Protestant-Jewish Seminarians' Program, one Presbyterian student said: "I am convicted that I want my children to grow up differently in the world, unafraid and engaged with all people, no matter their religion, culture, or socioeconomic location." A rabbinical student said: "How can I talk about Israel's contributions to the world when I do not even know one Muslim who lives in the Jewish state . . .

Ms. Julie Johnson-Staples and Rabbi Justus Baird discuss issues as part of the Protestant-Jewish Seminarians' program.

and I do not even have one Christian friend? There is a gap between my deepest conviction and the way I live my life."

Recently, Auburn launched a pilot program bringing together sixteen Christian and Jewish seminary students from the New York City area for classroom study and a trip to Israel and the West Bank. The program's purpose is to prepare emerging religious leaders with an understanding of what Israel/Palestine means to Christians, Jews, and Muslims; to experience the complex and multiple perspectives of each group; and to strengthen their relationships to each other as committed Christians and Jews.

Like young Solomon in the verse from 1 Kings, so too our future religious leaders ask God for wisdom, an understanding mind, and the ability to discern what is right as they wrestle with the challenges of the Israeli-Palestinian conflict in the region that Christians, Jews, and Muslims all call home.

—*Katharine Rhodes Henderson, president, Auburn Theological Seminary*

Prayer

God of all creation, give us open minds and humble hearts that we may learn of your surprising love and grace for all your peoples the world over. Use our voices, hands, and feet to do the hard work of making peace so that one day all will know the safety and security you intend. In the name of the Prince of Peace. Amen.

Sunday Lectionary and Hymns

Jer. 31:7–14
God, Our Help and Constant Refuge
PH 192

Ps. 147:12–20
Now Praise the Lord
PH 255

Eph. 1:3–14
Here, O Lord, Your Servants Gather
PH 465

John 1:(1–9) 10–18
Thanks to God Whose Word Was Written
PH 331

Daily Lectionary
☼ Ps. 111, 150 ☾ Ps. 107, 15
1 Kings 3:5–14
Col. 3:12–17; John 6:41–47

Let us join in prayer for:

Presbytery Staff
Elder Jim Bellatti, executive presbyter

PC(USA) General Assembly Staff
Elder Loyda Aja, OGA
Ben Albers, GAMC
Jeanette Andersen, BOP

Cimarron Presbytery

Oklahoma

Let the little children come to me, and do not hinder them, for the kingdom of God belongs to such as these" (Mark 10:14).

Each Sunday morning the First Presbyterian Church bus drives throughout Blackwell to pick up children whose parents don't usually attend church and takes them to Sunday school and church. On Sunday afternoon the church bus

Servants of Christ and King's Kids of Blackwell First Presbyterian Church volunteer at a car wash to raise funds for Dwight Mission.

Sheri Dittmann

is back on the road taking children and youth to afternoon fellowship and fun, followed by supper prepared by church volunteers. In this congregation of 106 members, 10–12 volunteers work with 20–40 children and youth each Sunday. The children are known as the King's Kids, and the youth, recognizing their call to service, refer to themselves as Servants of Christ. Because of this ministry commitment 30 percent to 50 percent of those attending worship each Sunday are children and youth. The number at King's Kids and Servants of Christ is maintained because these children and youth want to be in church and a part of the church family.

King's Kids and Servants of Christ give the children and youth of Blackwell a sense of belonging and of ownership, and a church they can call home. As Servants of Christ, the youth lead Sunday worship once or twice each year and frequently contribute to worship with songs of praise and adoration. The highlight of each year is a week of camp at Dwight Mission. Through the generosity of the members of First Presbyterian Church, and with the assistance of Cimarron Presbytery and Dwight Mission, full camp scholarships were provided to forty-one children and youth in the last three years.

Cimarron Presbytery's 15 churches have 2,312 members.

Prayer
Loving God, thank you for the volunteers who work countless hours to bring your word to the children of this world. Help us learn the ways to reach more of your people so that they may experience your unending love. In the name of your most holy Son, Jesus Christ. Amen.

Daily Lectionary
☼ Ps. 20, 145 ☾ Ps. 93, 97
Josh. 3:14—4:7
Eph. 5:1–20; John 9:1–12, 35–38

Eastern Oklahoma Presbytery

Congregations in Eastern Oklahoma Presbytery are deeply committed to ministries of service in their communities. First Presbyterian Church in Sapulpa has extended its Lend A Hand days from two a year to an ongoing ministry to those who need help with minor home repairs, yardwork, or whatever is needed, whenever it is needed. First Presbyterian Church in Bartlesville partners with community

Eastern Oklahoma Presbytery Youth Council leads an activity at a youth retreat.

organizations through its car repair ministry and Project Transformation, a summer literacy program for children. At College Hill Presbyterian Church, Spanish and English worship services are held simultaneously and worshipers celebrate Communion together. Several congregations partner or "adopt" elementary schools to provide tutoring and school supplies or help teachers with classroom supplies.

Young disciples continue to participate in programs at Dwight Mission Camp & Retreat Center. An annual Confirmation Retreat supplements existing confirmation courses and is a springboard for congregations beginning confirmation. The presbytery's Youth Council leads many events at Dwight for junior and senior youth.

Leadership development continues to be a priority throughout the presbytery in programs through the Lay Academy. Participants are not only developing new skills, but many have found a particular ministry within their own congregations. Twenty lay preachers currently serve in the presbytery, and twelve more are commissioned lay pastors.

The presbytery has 69 congregations with 9,371 members. Within its bounds are Presbyterian-related University of Tulsa and Goodland Academy.

Prayer

Loving God, you have blessed us with faithful, compassionate people who reach out to their neighbors with glad and generous hearts. Let us continue to have ears to hear and eyes to see the needs around us and to respond in love. Amen.

Let us join in prayer for:

Elder Gordon Nielsen, member, GAMC

Presbytery Staff
Rev. Dr. Gregory J. Coulter, general presbyter
Rev. Marcus Barber, associate general presbyter
Paul Merrill, pastor, The Journey new church development
Dana Bailey, stated clerk
Julie Burton, director of congregational resources
Teresa Herleth, administrative assistant
Jane Probey, financial secretary

PC(USA) General Assembly Staff
Joelle Anderson, GAMC
Monty Anderson, PPC

Daily Lectionary
☼ Ps. 99, 146 ☾ Ps. 96, 110
Jonah 2:2–9
Eph. 6:10–20; John 11:17–27, 38–44

Let us join in prayer for:

PC(USA) General Assembly Staff
Maria Arroyo, GAMC
Luke Asikoye, GAMC

Epiphany of the Lord

Minute for Mission

We have come from the east, west, north, south, and center of this country, but our ancestry spans the globe. We are people of many colors and ages. We are the PW Racial Ethnic Dialog, and we have been gathering once a year since 1998. In 2009 we are gathering in Louisville.

A Korean American elder, In Soon Chi, stands to lead our first devotion. She tells us how inadequately prepared she feels about her devotion and then says, "Of course, we Koreans have to always first apologize," and I finish the sentence with her. She and I burst out in knowing laughter.

The PW Racial Ethnic Dialog has been gathering since 1998.

It is now the last day of our time together. Lisione da Silva, a member of the group originally from Brazil, is about to lead a morning devotion. She tells us about how she too feels so unprepared because Brazilians do not worship with an elaborate written liturgy as "Americans" do. Miriam Murthy, a Filipina American member interjects loudly, "But you are not Korean!" This time, everybody bursts out laughing. We have all understood each other across our differences!

Matthew 12:21 sings of Jesus as God's servant in whom "the Gentiles will hope." The Greek word for "Gentiles" means "nations." Indeed, the Dialog is a gathering of the Gentiles. When we gather as a Dialog, our hope to become a beloved community is born and reborn in Jesus Christ. In moments like the one described above, God reveals God-self as the God of Gentiles.

—*Rev. Unzu Lee, program associate, Presbyterian Women, General Assembly Ministry Council*

Prayer

God of many colors, we draw near your servant Jesus in whom we have seen your promise of justice to the Gentiles fulfilled. In Jesus, who welcomed the strangers and rendered justice to the marginalized, we have seen God. May we, people of many colors living in this nation, find hope in this Jesus and see your face in each other. Amen.

Daily Lectionary
☼ Ps. 72, 147:1–11 ☾ Ps. 100, 67
Isa. 49:1–7
Rev. 21:22–27; Matt. 12:14–21

Grace Presbytery

Texas

In 2002 First Presbyterian Church of Temple made the decision to remain in its changing downtown area, and received a presbytery grant to develop spaces surrounding the building. As a part of the project, the youth requested a single basketball goal, which the church erected. Neighborhood youth came to the corner of First and French at all hours to shoot hoops with friends. Eventually one young man accepted an invitation to come inside.

The basketball goal has helped to develop rewarding relationships in the neighborhood.

He brought his brothers and sisters to the church's vacation Bible school. Other children followed for after-school programs and Sunday school.

Growing into this gift has not been easy. The church is learning to change to meet the needs of children who have never been to church or heard the stories. One little girl spied a picture of Jesus and asked, "Does he work here?" Another quiet young girl went home bubbling with enthusiasm, asking her family, "Do you know about Joseph? Let me tell you a story."

First Presbyterian's downtown neighborhood is facing many problems. The church is learning that the solution does not lie in the phrase "build it and they will come," but rather in the complicated and consistent process of learning names and building relationships.

Presbyterians in Grace Presbytery serve many ministries, including Presbyterian Children's Homes and Services, Austin College, and Presbyterian-related Camp Gilmont. These ministries are supported by 42,646 members in 177 congregations and several new church developments and fellowships.

Prayer

Ever present God, remind us daily that you have plans for us. Inspire us to walk even as Christ walked, going on our way in faith and gladness. Sharpen our spiritual vision that we may recognize the opportunities for ministry that you lay before us, and embolden us to act upon them with courage, opening ourselves to others along the way. Amen.

Let us join in prayer for:

Elder Carol J. Adcock, member, GAMC

Presbytery Staff
Rev. Marvin Groote, interim general presbyter
Elder Connie Tubb, stated clerk
Elder Sheryl Taylor, director, COM services
Kathy Sanders, assistant, COM services
Becky Robles, director, finance services
Carolyn Wyatt, director, church development
Rob Allen, director, communication services
Gwen Payne, administrative assistant
Elder Margaret LaPlante, administrative assistant
Esther Lee, assistant, finance services

PC(USA) General Assembly Staff
Charles Austin, FDN
Michelle Avery, GAMC

Daily Lectionary

☼ Ps. 46 *or* 97, 147:12–20
☾ Ps. 27, 93, *or* 114
Deut. 8:1–3
Col. 1:1–14; John 6:30–33, 48–51

Let us join in prayer for:

Presbytery Staff
Aaron Carland, general presbyter
Donna Giles, resource center director
Jack Huntress, stated clerk
Lauri Johnson, accountant

PC(USA) General Assembly Staff
Karen Babik, BOP
Dawn Baccare, BOP

Indian Nations Presbytery

Oklahoma

Greystone Presbyterian Church is an energized and growing congregation in north Oklahoma City. Founded in 1942, the church grew for its first twenty years. But by the late 1970s social unrest and a downturn in the oil business began to take a toll. Membership dwindled and enthusiasm waned—until 2004. With encouragement from the presbytery and caring pastoral leadership, the church began a new chapter in its ministry.

Upon completing a mission study in 2005 the congregation committed itself to reconnect with its changing neighborhood and discover the mission field at its doorstep. With a new designated pastor, Greystone has embarked on an ambitious strategy of redevelopment, revitalization, and transformation. Meanwhile, the Village/Nichols Hills area that surrounds the church is undergoing a similar transformation.

For Greystone "Growing Christ's Church Deep and Wide" is first about relationships—about meeting Christ and their neighbors. The congregation is rediscovering the joy of sharing the gospel, recovering a passion for evangelism that had marked its beginnings. With an increasing number of unchurched and under-churched people moving into the neighborhood, the congregation has found its mission field. These Presbyterians are finding new ways to get acquainted—becoming neighbors to those around the church, and hosting picnics and games on the church lawn.

"Growing Christ's Church Deep and Wide" is also about personal transformation, gaining new awareness of what it means to be Christ's faithful disciples. Following Jesus is a life-changing experience. Members seek to deepen their understanding of God's baptismal grace through joyful worship, earnest prayer, disciplined study, and engaging fellowship.

Greystone is finding new energy and excitement—learning daily what it means to live into Christ's promise: "Remember, I am with you always, to the end of the age" (Matt. 28:20).

Indian Nations Presbytery has 54 churches with 9,376 members.

Daily Lectionary

☼ Ps. 46 *or* 47, 148 ☾ Ps. 27, 93 *or* 114
Exod. 17:1–7
Col. 1:15–23; John 7:37–52

Prayer

Eternal God, you never fail to give us each day all that we ever need. Give us such joy in living and such peace in serving Christ that we may gratefully make use of all your blessings and joyfully seek our risen Lord in everyone we meet. In Jesus Christ we pray. Amen.

Mission Presbytery

Texas

Presbyterians are a connectional people: connected to God, each other, and God's creation. Churches have a commitment to due process, consensus building, and transparency. These are the values that informed Elder John Donahue to become a stakeholder in local efforts to ensure that the Edwards Aquifer in central Texas is managed in keeping with the biblical values of stewardship and respect for all God's creatures. Believing that God's Spirit continually flows

Mission Presbytery youth enjoy the crystal clear, spring-fed waters of John Knox Ranch in the Texas Hill Country.

through all things, John found himself in a wide and varied group of fellow stakeholders, all of whom shared a common concern for the environment. Even though they shared a devotion to this cause, many were estranged from one another due to years of disputes and conflicts over how best to use water from the aquifer while respecting federally recognized endangered species. Nonetheless, this diverse group came together seeking a way to reconcile their varied water interests and hoping to find a way to meet the needs of all and protect the aquifer itself.

Through extended social contact and sharing their values in an atmosphere of mutual respect, group members began to work through their disputes and feelings of distrust. John could see the Spirit at work among the stakeholders as together they learned the value of consensus building and mutual respect when the issues became potentially divisive. Just as the water runs throughout the land, so does the hope that the Spirit will continue to flow through this diverse group of people as they continue their guardianship of this resource.

Mission Presbytery is home to 31,283 members in 151 congregations.

Prayer

Jesus said we are to be the leaven in the bread, not the bread itself. Lord, as we find ourselves in groups of men and women of goodwill, help us to see your Spirit at work, to praise and thank you and to witness through our participation in human endeavors that your redeeming love is at work among us. Amen.

Let us join in prayer for:

Elder Esperanza Guajardo, member, GAMC

Presbytery Staff
Hilary Shuford, executive presbyter
Susan Penrod, associate presbyter, education and nurture
Miles White, stated clerk
Ruben Armendariz, consultant for church development
Martha Flores, administrative assistant/office manager
Lynne Powell, administrative assistant
Pam DuBois, accountant
Melani Cobb, receptionist/account assistant
Karen Black, Austin resource center director
Sandy Pinaire, Corpus Christi resource center director
Gayle Sharpley, San Antonio resource center director, director of communications
Lita Simpson, Valley resource center, youth ministry director
Sam Riccobene, outdoor ministries
Charlotte Hains, lay leadership institute

PC(USA) General Assembly Staff
Rev. Ernesto Badillo, BOP
Elder Joey Bailey, GAMC

Daily Lectionary

✿ Ps. 46 *or* 47, 149 ☾ Ps. 27, 93 *or* 114
Isa. 45:14–19
Col. 1:24—2:7; John 8:12–19

The Lord's Day

Minute for Mission: Baptism of the Lord

You are my Son, the Beloved; with you I am well pleased" (Luke 3:22). These tender words resounded in heaven and throughout the earth on the day when Jesus was baptized by John in the Jordan. On that day the heavens were opened, the Holy Spirit descended like a dove, and God's amazing grace was poured out upon the world.

God speaks the same words to each of us today: "You are my beloved child; with you I am well pleased." By the grace of God, we share our baptism with Jesus Christ, who has made us heirs of the promise, children of the covenant, members of Christ's body. This great good news is the wellspring of Christian life, the fountain of every imaginable blessing, the source of our holy calling, and a never-failing spring of hope and joy. In Christ we are God's beloved children—delivered from death, restored to new life, washed clean of our sin, and called to live as faithful disciples, sharing the story of our salvation and working for God's promised realm of justice and peace.

Presbyterians are rediscovering the deep significance of the Sacrament of Baptism in Christian life. The 2006 study *Invitation to Christ* encouraged congregations to explore a few simple sacramental practices—among them, to place the baptismal font in full view of the congregation, to keep it open and full of water every Sunday, and to lead certain parts of the service of worship from the font. With the font once again at the center of our common life, we have a renewed understanding of our baptism in Christ as the heart of Christian identity, the soul of Christian unity, and the strength of Christian vocation. Every stream of the church's mission and ministry can be traced to that abundant and abiding source—the grace of God, poured out in love for the world through Jesus Christ.

—*Rev. David Gambrell, associate for worship, General Assembly Mission Council*

Prayer
We praise you, God from whom all blessings flow, for the gift and calling of our baptism in Jesus Christ. Continue to pour out your Holy Spirit upon the church, so that we may be living water for a thirsty world; through Christ our Savior. Amen.

The Presbytery of New Covenant

Texas

The senior pastor of Grace Presbyterian Church in Houston felt a nudge from the Holy Spirit to challenge his congregation to invest in God's kingdom on earth. "In a time of financial uncertainty," says the Rev. Doug Ferguson, "we wanted to do something that would demonstrate that our trust is not in worldly wealth but in a God who richly provides."

An anonymous gift provided seed money. Each member who took the challenge to invest $100 was given

Eight-year-old Travis talks to Joseph Benson of Search Homeless Services to learn how his Kingdom investment would bless others and honor God.

three conditions: the money is God's, not yours; invest it in a way that expands God's kingdom on earth and blesses others; and report what you did. Among the amazing stories that were reported was Karen's, who felt God nudging her to invest in kids who had lost everything to Hurricane Ike. She raised over $36,000 to buy a new winter coat for every student at Ball High School in Galveston. Sharon bought the ingredients for baking the perfect cake, made and sold the cakes, and used the money to pay for tests of medical equipment donated to Project Cure that will be used in war-torn nations. Jenny learned that foot care is among the great struggles of the homeless. She launched her own ministry, Soul Care, to provide shoes, socks, foot ointment, and a New Testament for homeless people. Bob knew that a domestic worker in his neighborhood was struggling to pay for a plane ticket for her son's graduation from U.S. Marine Corps basic training. He raised $1,000 to pay for the trip that brought mother and son together.

The Presbytery of New Covenant serves 107 churches with 36,920 members.

Prayer

Thank you, gracious God, for allowing us to experience your love, hope, and provision in our lives and in the lives of our neighbors. May we always be available to your call to serve others, sensitive to your Holy Spirit, and grateful for the great love you have shown us through your Son, Jesus Christ. Amen.

Let us join in prayer for:

Presbytery Staff
Rev. Mike Cole, general presbyter
Rev. Wendy Bailey, associate general presbyter for evangelism/renewal and new church development
Elder Mary Marcotte, associate general presbyter for discipleship and leadership development
Rev. Diane Prevary, stated clerk
Elder Forbes Baker, director of business affairs and finance
Patricia Brantley, database coordinator/receptionist
Elder Sharon Darden, coordinator for COM and CPM
Sandra Lopez, assistant for finance and administration
Elder Janice Schessler, coordinator for administrative, constitutional, and ecclesiastical relations
Elder Carrie Walker, coordinator of conferences and graphics
Elder Helen Wolf, editor
Scott Young, webmaster
Rev. Mary Currie, volunteer in mission

PC(USA) General Assembly Staff
Marsha Bailey, GAMC
Hollis Baker, BOP

Daily Lectionary

☼ Ps. 5, 145 ☾ Ps. 82, 29
Gen. 2:4–9 (10–15) 16–25
Heb. 1:1–14; John 1:1–18

Daily Lectionary
☼ Ps. 42, 146 ☾ Ps. 102, 133
Gen. 3:1–24
Heb. 2:1–10; John 1:19–28

Palo Duro Presbytery

Texas

Matthews Memorial Presbyterian Church (MMPC) is located in the vibrant, historical town of Albany, which *Texas Monthly* magazine has called "the best small town in Texas." Albany may be small, but at MMPC one is quickly reminded that our big God is definitely at work there.

In recent years, MMPCs membership and worship attendance have increased significantly. With this growth has come a need to expand both the perspective of the members of Matthews' congregation on what God is doing in their midst and the physical structures from which they will do ministry. MMPC has completed a $1.4-million project that renovated its existing space and added bathrooms, classrooms, a nursery, a quiet room, and a youth room. MMPC was blessed to construct this new wing without incurring debt.

The 3,884-square-foot addition to Matthews Memorial's educational wing was under construction in 2009.

This is news worth celebrating because of everything the Lord has done. As the Rev. Trey H. Little, pastor of MMPC, remarked, "This is the result of our big God once again doing more than we could possibly imagine. This is all about the transforming work of Jesus Christ and his willingness to give this body of Christ even more opportunity to reach this community for the glory of God."

"What about you?" the Rev. Little continues. "Are you looking for God at work in your midst? Are you capitalizing on God's desire to grow Christ's church deep and wide? Let your imagination run wild and let God remind you just how big God really is."

There are 53 congregations and 9,091 members within Palo Duro Presbytery.

Prayer

Gracious and mighty God, forgive us our lack of imagination and for underestimating what you can and will do in our lives and your church. Through your Holy Spirit, equip us with the power and passion to respond to you in love. Remind us yet again that your grace in Jesus Christ is more than sufficient. Thank you for your faithfulness and endless provision. May we daily lean on your everlasting arms. Amen.

The Presbytery of the Pines

Arkansas, Louisiana

The first fruits of almost two years of preparation became a reality in October 2008 with the installation of two water purification systems in the towns of Gonaïves and Gros Morne, Haiti. Joining efforts of Living Waters for the World, a Pines mission team was formed that was spearheaded by Karen and Danny Logan, elders from Belcher (Louisiana) Presbyterian Church. On this trip were four members from the Presbytery of the Pines—Webb Sentell, John Guice, Karen, and Danny—as well as Chris and Ruthie McRae from the Presbytery of Arkansas and Germantown Presbyterian Church members Chris Ham, Leigh Powers, Lanny Oakes, and Bill Armstrong.

While some of the team concentrated on the water system installation, other team members taught children, their teachers, community leaders, and parents the importance of clean water, basic health and hygiene lessons, and stories from the Bible illustrating the gift of living water for all God's people.

An important aspect of each water installation was the spiritual component shared by those who spent the week together. The team worked together with Haitian friends, shared prayers at their meals together each day, and worshiped at their church on Sunday. After sharing Communion, the team found friendships developing more deeply and learned more about the challenges Haitians face as they try to feed and clothe their families. Team members listened to their new friends' hopes for their country and desires for their families, and came to better understand their feelings of helplessness.

In the words of team member Karen Logan, "These trips to Haiti have helped me change my attitude, rearrange my value system and my priorities, and become more tolerant, more patient, and, I hope, more sensitive to the needs of others."

Evergreen Ministries, a ministry to people with disabilities, and Vera Lloyd Home for Children, a ministry for children on difficult life journeys, are two specialized ministries within the presbytery.

The 63 churches in the Presbytery of the Pines have 5,574 members.

Prayer

Open the sleepy eyes of the wealthy nations, Lord. Awaken us from our overfed slumber to responsibility for our needy brothers and sisters. Teach us again how much we have that we do not need, and how much they need that they do not have. Amen.

Let us join in prayer for:

Presbytery Staff
Rev. Joe Hill, general presbyter
Cindy Sandifer, information services

PC(USA) General Assembly Staff
Kay Ballard, GAMC
Alan Barthel, PAM

Daily Lectionary
☼ Ps. 89:1–18, 147:1–11 ☾ Ps. 1, 33
Gen. 4:1–16
Heb. 2:11–18; John 1:(29–34) 35–42

The Presbytery of South Louisiana

During Hurricane Rita in 2005 St. Andrew's Presbyterian Church in Lake Charles was heavily damaged: a large, stained-glass window shattered, allowing wind and water to destroy the interior. On February 8, 2009, the church—rebuilt and alive—celebrated its fiftieth anniversary.

During that day's service the "Rita cross," a collaboration between Elder Raymond Clawson and stained-glass artist Frank Thompson, was dedicated. Elder Clawson's prayer of dedication closed with the affirmation, "Trusting in Jesus Christ, we dedicate this cross in the name of the Father, and the Son, and the Holy Spirit." The simple cross, made from the broken glass of the Rita-shattered window, rests upon a firm foundation of native cypress timber.

The pieces of dark stained glass banded together are a reminder of how the storm elicited the connecting love and unity of the Presbyterian Church (U.S.A.) and brought people together from St. Andrew's, the local area, the state, and across the nation to help put the pieces of the church back together. A band of brass holds the pieces together, signifying God's embracing love. No matter how diverse in size, shape, and thought, all are the body of Christ.

In the center of the cross is a triangle—a symbol of the Trinity—of red glass. The rough and broken red glass surface is a reminder that Jesus' short ministry had rough, hard times and represents the blood shed for us. A candle mounted behind the cross produces light that shines through the dark glass and the red Trinity glass as a reminder of God's presence and light shining through the witness of his people. The people of St. Andrew's, led by commissioned lay pastor Nanette Cagney, look forward to following the Rita cross into the future.

The 61 churches in the Presbytery of South Louisiana have 6,862 members.

Prayer
Gracious God, thank you for the faithfulness of your people who seek to turn calamity into beauty and shards into wholeness. Remind us to honor your life-giving Spirit in all whom we encounter today. In Jesus' name. Amen.

The Presbytery of Tres Rios

Texas

Let us join in prayer for:

Presbytery Staff
Rev. Jose Luis Casal, general missioner
Rev. Patty Lane, stated clerk
Jimmy Stevens, treasurer
Theresa Wright, administrative assistant

PC(USA) General Assembly Staff
Elder Beth Basham, GAMC
Danella Bass, FDN
Terri Bate, GAMC

In late September 2008 the border towns of Presidio, Texas, and Ojinaga, Mexico, in a region where the annual rainfall averages ten inches, were inundated by floodwaters due to torrential rains.

At that time most emergency response personnel had their hands full dealing with the aftermath of Hurricane Ike on the Texas Gulf Coast.

Nevertheless, the two closest Presbyterian churches—First, Alpine, and First, Marfa—gathered and delivered immediate relief to victims on both sides of the Rio Grande.

Other churches of the Presbytery of Tres Rios contributed financially to assist in the relief efforts. The Rev. Jobeth McLeod, pastor of First Presbyterian Church, Alpine, has administered these funds. In partnership with the Big Bend Frontera mission, this assistance is being used to reestablish farmland on the Mexico side. Alfalfa fields along the river were washed out and covered in silt from the flooding and can be reclaimed only through extensive efforts, beyond the means of many area farmers. Contributions that are raised are being used to purchase tractor fuel, which will enable farmers in the Ojinaga area to replant in the spring and carry on their livelihood.

Presbyterians helped Presidio residents recover from flooding in 2008.

Other funds were used to purchase food and to make repairs at Casa Hogar, an orphanage in Ojinaga supported by several churches of the presbytery.

The Presbytery of Tres Rios has 33 churches serving 6,732 members. It provides annual support for mission projects Project Vida and Pasos de Fe in El Paso, St. Andrews Mission in Midland, and Project Dignidad in San Angelo.

Prayer

Gracious God, you have called us to a life of service. You have asked that we hear the voice of Jesus in the cries of our sisters and brothers who hunger and thirst. Give us the power to turn their hunger into fullness and their thirst into satisfaction that they may know the power of their God. Let us be your servants, serving them with love and grace. Amen.

Daily Lectionary

☼ Ps. 51, 148 ☾ Ps. 142, 65
Gen. 6:1–8
Heb. 3:12–19; John 2:1–12

The Synod of the Trinity

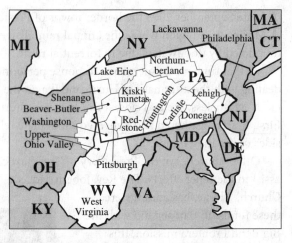

How does God call us to partnership in mission in a new world?" was the central question as leaders from the presbyteries gathered for a mission funding consultation early in 2009. From the event emerged a fascinating mix of ideas and responses as to how to do ministry and mission as a dynamic part of the PC(USA).

The participants shared responses ranging from "better interpretation of mission" to "building relationships" to "helping the whole church catch an entrepreneurial spirit." They reviewed in depth the ordination questions answered by the ministers of Word and Sacrament, elders, and deacons, which reminded them how those vows focus on their ministry together.

James Vandeberg, representing the General Assembly Mission Council, elaborated on realities of mission and funding: a low level of awareness of Presbyterian mission, a preference for designated gifts, and a lack of understanding in mission giving.

After the consultation some participants expressed a need for something concrete with which to better articulate the current status of synod/presbytery connections. Others were pleased to have tools to better seek ways to keep the conversation alive with passion, and as a vital witness to the fact that we are, indeed, the body of Christ.

The Synod of the Trinity consists of 16 presbyteries, 1,269 congregations, 245,532 Presbyterians, 7 Presbyterian Church (U.S.A.)-related colleges, and Pittsburgh Theological Seminary.

Prayer

Lord God, you call us to come and to not be afraid. You tell us to go and to not be afraid. You promise to be with us in our coming and going, and for that we thank you. May our lives be a continual witness of your love and mercy. Amen.

Daily Lectionary
☼ Ps. 104, 149 ☾ Ps. 138, 98
Gen. 6:9–22
Heb. 4:1–13; John 2:13–22

The Lord's Day

Minute for Mission: Race Relations

What is sacred about a sacred conversation about race? Everything! Our foundation is the affirmation that God has created and loves each of us as a child of God. Like all of creation the human family represents an abundant and amazing diversity, yet each of us is created in the image of God. We are called to be members of the body of Christ and to share our gifts for the good of the body and the glory of God. As the body of Christ, the church is called to give testimony to the universality of God's love. Yet too often, the gifts of some individuals and communities are not valued or nurtured, and people labeled "different" find they have no voice or place to share the gifts that God has given them.

Race continues to divide and alienate us. Race is still a major factor that affects economic status, educational achievement, political power, health, even prison rates. The reality of racism is a scandal to the gospel and a mortal wound in the body of Christ. Acknowledging this, the United Church of Christ invited communities of faith to engage in sacred conversations on race—to confront the realities of race in our society and take intentional steps to dismantle racism in the church and in the world.

The Belhar Confession is one resource on which to build a sacred conversation on race. In 2004 the 216th General Assembly urged all Presbyterians to study this confession, which arose out of the experience of racism and apartheid in South Africa. In 2008 the 218th General Assembly created a task force to study the Belhar Confession—the first step to considering adding the confession to our own *Book of Order*. A study guide is available at pcusa.org/theologyandworship/confession.htm.

In the words of the Belhar Confession, "God has entrusted the church with the message of reconciliation in and through Jesus Christ . . . to be the salt of the earth and the light of the world, . . . [a] witness both by word and by deed to the new heaven and the new earth in which righteousness dwells."

—*Rev. Teresa Chávez Sauceda, minister member-at-large,*
Presbytery of San Francisco

Prayer

How precious is your steadfast love, O God! Let your perfect love cast out all fear of the "other" and let your Spirit inspire us with courage, wisdom, and imagination to dismantle the racism that divides and dehumanizes us. Guide us, nurture us, mold us, that we might be faithful witnesses to your abundant love. Amen.

Sunday Lectionary and Hymns

Isa. 62:1–5
Glorious Things of Thee Are Spoken
PH 446, HB 434

Ps. 36:5–10
Thy Mercy and Thy Truth, O Lord
PH 186, HB 82

1 Cor. 12:1–11
Come, Holy Spirit, Our Souls Inspire
PH 125, HB 237

John 2:1–11
Down to Earth, as a Dove
PH 300

Daily Lectionary

☼ Ps. 19, 150 ☾ Ps. 81, 113
Gen. 7:1–10, 17–23
Eph. 4:1–16; Mark 3:7–19

The Presbytery of Beaver-Butler

Pennsylvania

Let us join in prayer for:

Presbytery Staff
Rev. Alan Adams, executive presbyter
Rev. David Byers, stated clerk
Rev. Dennis Burnett, assistant stated clerk
James Gray, treasurer
Rev. Connie Dunn, presbytery moderator
James Powers, presbytery vice-moderator
Mike Helms, coordinating
team chairperson
Sidney Fisher, resource center director
Lauren Cesnales, accountant
Barbara Paff, secretary to the
executive presbyter
Mary Clow, secretary to the units
and committees

PC(USA) General Assembly Staff
Elder Morton Bell, OGA
Serrita Bell, FDN

A mbridge . . . Jefferson Center . . . Crestview . . . Butler. A roll call of the 86 churches and 14,581 members in the Presbytery of Beaver-Butler would find each community engaged in ministries—food pantries, community dinners, basketball clinics, God's Acres, and more.

Members of the Maanaim Church, Belo Horizonte, Brazil, visit their partners at Mill Creek Presbyterian Church in Hookstown.

Slidell . . . Mexico City . . . Gulfport . . . Haiti . . . South Africa. Mission teams carry the Water of Life to these and many other places each year. A mission trip to Slidell, Louisiana, in February 2009 included thirteen people from the presbytery's small churches.

Nicaragua . . . Sri Lanka . . . China . . . Philippines . . . Russia . . . Republic of South Africa. These are a few of the countries in which PC(USA) missionaries are supported by churches in the presbytery. In response to Mission Challenge '07, every congregation chose a PC(USA) missionary as its special prayer concern. Over 50 percent of the churches now support one or more mission workers with prayer, letters, or financial gifts.

Brazil . . . Mexico . . . Romania . . . Kenya . . . Dominican Republic . . . Malawi. Sixteen congregations now have ongoing international partnerships with churches in one of these countries.

God's Spirit is moving in quiet and powerful ways in the lives of the congregations. A woman from Highland Church invited a friend from Unionville Church to come with her on a mission trip. The friend in turn invited others from her congregation to join the group—and now there is a lively and involved mission committee in that church. This is how the commitment to mission is growing within and among Presbyterian churches: one person sharing enthusiasm for mission with another.

Prayer
God, keep us ever aware of the ways in which you guide, sustain, challenge, and empower us, day by day. Let your word be springs of water flowing through the church to thirsty souls worldwide. Amen.

Daily Lectionary
✿ Ps. 135, 145 ☾ Ps. 97, 112
Gen. 8:6–22
Heb. 4:14—5:6; John 2:23—3:15

The Presbytery of Carlisle

Pennsylvania

Churches within the Presbytery of Carlisle have been involved in ministry in Honduras for many years. Gettysburg Presbyterian makes an annual medical mission trip to Honduras, and Second Presbyterian, Carlisle, has made trips with Heifer International through PC(USA) missionaries Gloria and Tim Wheeler. Falling Spring Presbyterian in Chambersburg is building a school in northern Honduras, and Market Square Presbyterian and the orphanage El Hogar in Tegucigalpa have had a long-standing relationship.

The partnership between the presbyteries of Carlisle and Honduras began in 2006 when members of Christ Presbyterian in Camp Hill became interested in sending a medical mission team.

Since then the presbytery's involvement in Honduras has grown each year. Mission trips to Honduras have included church members from at least five churches. The children of St. Andrews, Lebanon, gave money toward Bibles for children in Honduras. Christ Presbyterian assembled health kits for workers in the small villages of Honduras. Mechanicsburg Presbyterian gave money and sent a construction team to build a new church building in Nacaome.

Members from Christ Presbyterian Church in Camp Hill prepare to leave for a medical clinic in Honduras.

All who have been involved in Honduras have returned home strengthened in their faith, in awe of the determination of the Presbyterian clergy and lay leaders in Honduras. Mark Englund-Krieger is now the moderator of the Honduras Mission Network.

The presbytery's 52 churches have 14,641 members.

Prayer

Loving God, help us to see beyond the limits of our work here at home. May we be open to new experiences, new callings, and new relationships at all times. As we share in your love in our own communities and around the world, may we be ever in awe of your rivers of living water, flowing together for your glory. In Jesus' name we pray. Amen.

Tuesday, January 19

Let us join in prayer for:

Presbytery Staff
Rev. Mark Englund-Krieger, executive presbyter
Suzanne Souder, associate for communication and office management
James Speedy, stated clerk

PC(USA) General Assembly Staff
Stewart Beltz, BOP
Cathy Benge, FDN
Bland Bennett, FDN

Daily Lectionary
☼ Ps. 123, 146 ☾ Ps. 30, 86
Gen. 9:1–17
Heb. 5:7–14; John 3:16–21

The Presbytery of Donegal

Pennsylvania

Let us join in prayer for:

Presbytery Staff
Rev. Charles W. Gross, Jr., acting executive presbyter and associate executive presbyter
Rev. Dr. William J. Brown, executive presbyter emeritus
Rev. Dr. William J. Netting, stated clerk
Kathy Bartels, administrative assistant
Susan Harner, business administrator and treasurer
Nan Best, associate for healthy congregations
Amy Wade, Camp Donegal administrator
Frederick Schmidt, hunger action enabler
Barbara Warren, restoring creation enabler
Betty Duncan, resource center director
Ann Mead Ash, newsletter editor

PC(USA) General Assembly Staff
Deborah Bernard, BOP
Rev. Dr. Jon Berquist, PPC

The Presbytery of Donegal has a passionate heart for mission and sends 50 percent of its mission money to the General Assembly. During a period of transition and self-examination Donegal designated 2008 "The Year of World Mission." The Rev. and Mrs. James Caldwell assembled a program of speakers, workshops, and events that gave the presbytery a new perspective on its connection to world mission. This focus led the presbytery to send a missionary family to be commissioned at the 218th General Assembly (2008) to go and serve the Lord. In the poverty-stricken region where they are ministering, they are experiencing God's blessings and lavish hospitality. In a powerful way, they are witnessing to the love of God in Jesus Christ. One young couple, Kevin and Jessica Crossan, responded to God's call by going to Northern Ireland as Young Adult Volunteers in mission in 2008–2009. According to the Crossans, "This is where God has called us for this year. We realize his plan has worked out much better than our own would have. We run a youth fellowship, help out in a nursery program and an after-school program, and teach Bible studies." Alicia Weber heard God's call during her last semester of college. She had been to New Orleans on a mission trip and knew that she was being called back to this work. She says, "I decided to listen to God's call . . . and it has opened my life to so much joy—living for my Lord and serving his beloved children in spite of my flaws, fears, and discomfort." The presbytery is richly blessed by many passionate servants of Jesus Christ and takes delight in how God has called young and old to go into the world with the awesome news of life abundant and life eternal.

> *In a powerful way, they are witnessing to the love of God in Jesus Christ.*

The Presbytery of Donegal has 57 churches, 3 new church developments, and 21,070 members.

Daily Lectionary
☼ Ps. 15, 147:1–11 ☾ Ps. 48, 4
Gen. 9:18–29
Heb. 6:1–12; John 3:22–36

Prayer

Sovereign, holy, loving, gracious Lord God, continue to call us, shape us, equip us, and send us into the world as your witnesses! Bless all who serve you and witness to the grace and peace of Jesus Christ. Open us to your Spirit in new ways and open closed countries to your abundance, your love, and your grace. We pray this in the matchless name of Jesus Christ. Amen.

The Presbytery of Huntingdon

Pennsylvania

For over twenty years the Presbytery of Huntingdon has been involved in mission activities in Thailand. Today, mission interpreters Lance and Debbie Potter serve the community through the Chiang Mai International School (CMIS), where Lance has been the principal since July 2008. CMIS is related to the Church of Christ in Thailand, a PC(USA) partner.

The children enjoy a program at CMIS.

Betty Jo Potter

In a letter Lance wrote that one way they are making a difference is by affirming the value of young people even when they struggle. One senior was kicked out of school for academic troubles. Lance had taught him in sixth grade and knew his family background was unsettled. The administration let him return to school, and he is doing better academically, was the high point scorer in his age group at the conference track meet, and has a major part in the upcoming school musical. A ninth grader was adopted as a young girl by missionaries who run an AIDS orphanage. She is HIV positive and has struggled with health and academic issues. The school staff was able to create a special program for her, and now she is doing quite well. She sang a lovely solo, her first ever, at a Christmas concert.

In addition, Debbie supports a Burma relief effort by providing important organizational assistance and is active with students through an after-school tutoring program.

The Potters strive to show God's love by creating an atmosphere at CMIS that allows those involved—students, parents, and teachers—to serve and deepen their relationships after the example of Christ.

The Presbytery of Huntingdon has 50 churches and 6,342 members and is home to Krislund Camp and Conference Center.

Prayer

God of our lives, bless the learning that goes on at the Chiang Mai International School. May teachers, students, and families alike be enriched and nurtured. Thank you for the Potters and the good work they are doing there. In Christ's name we pray. Amen.

Let us join in prayer for:

Presbytery Staff
Joy Kaufmann, general presbyter
Virginia Rainey, stated clerk
Elizabeth Armstrong, administrative treasurer
JoAnn Kimmel, mission treasurer
Lynn Illingworth, pastoral care consultant
Marie Carlson, office assistant

PC(USA) General Assembly Staff
Shawn Berry, FDN
Barbara Betts, GAMC
Herbert Beverly, OGA

Daily Lectionary
☼ Ps. 36, 147:12–20 ☾ Ps. 80, 27
Gen. 11:1–9
Heb. 6:13–20; John 4:1–15

Let us join in prayer for:

Presbytery Staff
Rev. Wayne A. Yost, general presbyter
Rev. Erin Cox-Holmes, associate
general presbyter
Marilyn Tully, stated clerk
Holly Wadding, administrative assistant
Carol Mock, resource center and
duplication coordinator
Debbie Lundgren, treasurer

PC(USA) General Assembly Staff
Elder Beneva Bibbs, GAMC
Teresa Bidart, GAMC

Week of Prayer for Christian Unity

The Presbytery of Kiskiminetas

Pennsylvania

It was evident God was leading the congregation of Beechwoods Presbyterian Church to complete the Kabadaha Church in Rwanda. Initially, ten people from Beechwoods volunteered to gather per mile pledges to bicycle eighteen miles on the Clarion/Little Toby Trail. When they arrived early on that Saturday morning in September, it was a cold and rainy forty-two degrees. Gathered with pledge sheets were twenty-four bicyclists ages eleven through seventy-six from Beechwoods and beyond. Volunteers were ready to supply fruit and drinks on the trail, and paramedics and an ambulance were standing

All twenty-four bicyclists completed the eighteen-mile "Ride to Raise a Roof in Rwanda."

by. Members of the congregation were busy preparing a luncheon to be served upon completion of this "Ride to Raise a Roof in Rwanda."

After asking for God's protection and blessing, the flag was dropped and peddling began. Even bundled up the bicyclists were cold, but the fellowship, laughter, and magnificent view of God's beautiful nature warmed their hearts and bodies.

Three hours later, when the last of the twenty-four bicyclists crossed that finish line and a sign displayed pledges totaling $6,044, they were revitalized by the knowledge that a new sanctuary would be constructed more than 10,000 miles away! Within five months, Beechwoods had raised $14,500. The Kabadaha Presbyterian Church now sits on a mountainside in Rwanda, dedicated to the honor and glory of our Lord and Savior, who walked and bicycled with them the entire ride.

The Presbytery of Kiskiminetas has 11,189 members in its 88 churches.

Prayer

Our gracious Heavenly Father, we thank you for instilling in our hearts the desire to serve those less fortunate. Thank you for showing us, Lord, that by serving others we are truly serving you. Please continue to work in us and through us to share your love. In the name of Jesus, we pray. Amen.

Daily Lectionary
☼ Ps. 130, 148 ☾ Ps. 32, 139
Gen. 11:27—12:8
Heb. 7:1–17; John 4:16–26

The Presbytery of Lackawanna

Pennsylvania

Members of First Presbyterian Church of Towanda began the ministry of Hezekiah's Hands in 2003. The group had participated in both regional and overseas mission trips and wanted to create similar opportunities for service closer to home. They found that many in Bradford County were in need of their help with home repairs.

Volunteers from Hezekiah's Hands provide practical help to neighbors in need.

"Mission Week" is set aside each June for repair projects. Before the work date each project is evaluated for the time required, size of the crew, materials, and skill level. Volunteers sign up to help on one or more days during the work week. Projects and people are matched based on the specific skills required. At least six churches from five denominations work together.

At 7:30 a.m. on Monday of the designated week, volunteers gather together, bringing tools, lunches, and lots of drinking water. After a time of prayer, volunteers are assigned to job sites where materials are assembled and everyone undertakes their mission. The work day ends in time for the crew to gather for a family meal and devotions at 5:00 p.m. Around the table, stories and joys are shared.

All of the funds for the projects are raised by Hezekiah's Hands, which helps anyone in need and at no cost. The group gives each homeowner a Bible signed by the crew who did the work. Hezekiah's Hands finds its motivation in Matthew 5:16, to let your light shine before others, so that they may see your good works and give glory to your Father in heaven.

The Presbytery of Lackawanna has 62 churches with 7,957 members.

Prayer

God of mission, we thank you for sending us the Savior and the Holy Spirit, who empower us for our mission. You have called each of us to leave our small world and go into the world of hurt and need. God of mission, provide for and bless the mission of Hezekiah's Hands and of the Presbytery of Lackawanna. Amen.

Saturday, January 23

Let us join in prayer for:

Rev. Susan J. Ezell, member, GAMC

Presbytery Staff
Rev. Dr. Barbara Ann Smith, general presbyter
Margaret Zeigler, administrative coordinator

PC(USA) General Assembly Staff
Melanie Biller, GAMC
Gail Bingham, GAMC
Michelle Bingham, GAMC

Daily Lectionary

☼ Ps. 56, 149 ☾ Ps. 118, 111
Gen. 12:9—13:1
Heb. 7:18–28; John 4:27–42

Sunday Lectionary and Hymns

Neh. 8:1–3, 5–6, 8–10
O Word of God Incarnate
PH 327, HB 251

Ps. 19
God's Law Is Perfect and Gives Light
PH 167
Most Perfect Is the Law of God
HB 257

1 Cor. 12:12–31a
In Christ There Is No East or West
PH 439, 440, HB 479

Luke 4:14–21
Live Into Hope
PH 332

The Lord's Day

Minute for Mission: Christian Unity

This summer will bring two great opportunities in the church ecumenical and in our own Reformed family to witness to the uniting power of God's Spirit. Our hope is that these opportunities will make us more determined to seek broader and deeper unity among all of God's people for a better and more just world.

June 2–6 in Edinburgh, Scotland, the church will commemorate the centenary of the World Missionary Conference, which started the modern ecumenical movement and, consequently, the establishment of the World Council of Churches.

June 18–28 in Grand Rapids, Michigan, the historic Uniting General Council will meet, when the World Alliance of Reformed Churches and the Reformed Ecumenical Council will unite to form the World Communion of Reformed Churches. Delegates will gather under the theme "Unity of the Spirit in the Bond of Peace."

In my own community I am working toward unity through an initiative I have called the Middlesex Quartet, an ecumenical mission partnership of our Presbyterian congregation and congregations from the Roman Catholic, Assemblies of God, and Southern Baptist traditions.

Abram and Lot, though kinsmen, found that the only way they could survive and thrive economically was to split. Little did they know that the Lord God had other plans. The reconciliation of family at the local level would bring all the nations from all corners of the earth in praise to the Lord.

—Rev. Neal D. Presa, pastor, Middlesex Presbyterian Church in Middlesex, New Jersey; convenor/chair, Caribbean and North American Area Council of the World Alliance of Reformed Churches (WARC); member, WARC Executive Committee

Daily Lectionary

☼ Ps. 67, 150 ☾ Ps. 46, 93
Gen. 13:2–18
Gal. 2:1–10; Mark 7:31–37

Prayer
Holy Spirit, forgive our tendency toward fight and flight. Heal our divisions, we pray, so that we may be one, just as Jesus Christ and the Father are one. Bless the gatherings this summer and throughout this year that seek to unite your people around the world and in our communities, to the praise and glory of God. Amen.

The Presbytery of Lake Erie

Pennsylvania

In February 2008 a member of Emmanuel Presbyterian Church in Erie looked around the church's dark and dusty basement, which was being used as a storage area. He knew that the space was not being utilized to its fullest potential, and he had an idea. He visualized an attractively decorated café where one day a week people could come to relax, listen to Christian music, fellowship, enjoy tasty snacks, and hear the word of God.

He described his idea to other church members, and soon they formed a committee to make the vision of a cozy and inviting courtyard setting a reality. The name was chosen immediately— Faith Café. The restoration work began enthusiastically and continued throughout that summer by numerous excited congregation members of all ages. With great anticipation opening night finally arrived, and it was a huge success!

Faith Café showcases a different local Christian band each week. The bands play two sets of music with a brief, uplifting message between the sets. The weekly attendance varies between 65 and 120 guests, from very young children to senior citizens. The feedback from the bands, guests, and congregation members has been very positive, and new visitors attend every week.

Musician's perform at Faith Café— Emmanuel Presbyterian Church, Erie.

James Breter

Faith Café is Emmanuel Presbyterian Church's gift, its outreach to the community, a safe and inviting, family-oriented atmosphere to bring people to a better understanding of Christ in a modern, nontraditional format. This exciting ministry is supported financially by the church as well as through a Bold New Initiative grant from the presbytery.

Emmanuel Presbyterian Church has approximately 166 members. The 60 churches in the Presbytery of Lake Erie have 10,602 members.

Prayer

Loving God, as the world seems to change around us so rapidly, lead us to share the life-changing message of Jesus Christ in new ways and in nontraditional settings. Through Jesus Christ. Amen.

Monday, January 25

Let us join in prayer for:

Elder Douglas F. Megill, member, GAMC

Presbytery Staff
Elder Douglas F. Megill, stated clerk
Rev. Dr. David S. Oyler III, general presbyter
Sheila Kelly, administrative assistant
Kerry Balzer, bookkeeper
William DeWitt, treasurer
Elaine Garts, resource center director
Jamie Fowler, Christian education director

PC(USA) General Assembly Staff
Michele Black, BOP
Anne Blair, GAMC

Daily Lectionary
☼ Ps. 57, 145 ☾ Ps. 85, 47
Gen. 14:(1–7) 8–24
Heb. 8:1–13; John 4:43–54

Lehigh Presbytery

Pennsylvania

Imagine an entire nation of churches whose Bibles and hymnals are so old they are held together by string. This was the case in Romania between the years after World War II and the fall of the dictator Nicolae Ceaușescu in 1989.

The Word of God literally dried up. In 1990 the Oradea diocese of the Hungarian Reformed Church bought a printing press and the Word began to flow again. But in 2007 the forty-year-old printing press failed. The Word of God dried up once more, leaving 350,000 believers without any new Bibles or hymnbooks. A new printing press would have cost $80,000.

Romania is the only European Union member without a national ecumenical council, and a much needed consultation series to establish an ecumenical council would have cost $30,000.

The Worldwide Ministries Care Team (WMCT) of Lehigh Presbytery has partnerships with both the Oradea and Cluj-Napoca dioceses in Romania, which together serve about one million believers. The WMCT provided a grant of over $18,000, most of which was used as a down payment toward restarting the printing press operation. The balance funded the first two meetings to advance the creation of the proposed Ecumenical Council of Romania, which will represent fifteen denominations.

When its forty-year-old printing press failed, the Hungarian Reformed Church of Romania found itself without Bibles and hymnbooks.

The WMCT primed the pump. Other partners have contributed matching funds for the printing press. The ecumenical council is being established. It began with one idea, one small committee, and one act of generous giving. It ended in one act of love that will impact millions of people.

Lehigh Presbytery is composed of 35 worshiping communities with 10,884 members and is home to Brainerd Presbyterian Center.

Prayer

Heavenly Father, let us release what is in our hands, planting seeds that when watered will bring forth new rivers of life and hope where tragedy and despair formerly reigned. In Jesus' name. Amen.

The Presbytery of Northumberland

Pennsylvania

E lijah's Bowl Community Soup Kitchen, whose name was inspired by God's faithfulness to the prophet Elijah and the generosity of the widow in 1 Kings 17, opened on January 26, 1991, in the fellowship hall of First Presbyterian Church, Sunbury. On that first Saturday eleven dear souls were fed. Through the grace of God and the faithful generosity of numerous churches, individuals, and community organizations, Elijah's Bowl has served more than 70,000 meals.

The coffeepot's always on at Elijah's Bowl.

Leaders are clear about the purpose of Elijah's Bowl: at lunchtime every Saturday, they address not only physical hunger, but people's need to be heard and to feel loved. Volunteers greet guests by their first names and offer compassion through a listening ear, a prayer, or the human touch of a hug, handshake, or a smile. Guests have developed friendships and a support network among themselves over the years.

Although originally an outreach of First Presbyterian Church, today churches of many denominations, civic groups, and students from a three-county area serve at Elijah's Bowl. With the guests they serve they experience God's Spirit of hope and the real and powerful presence of Jesus.

Canned goods, day-old bread, and pastries go home with guests to supplement their grocery needs. Some participate in monthly hymn sings or bimonthly cooking and nutrition classes. Because of friendships with members of First Presbyterian, Elijah's Bowl guests participate in the church's Christmas Live Nativity, an Easter egg hunt in a park, and in their own vacation Bible school class.

The Presbytery of Northumberland is home to 44 congregations with 5,345 members; Camp Krislund—a shared ministry of Carlisle, Huntingdon, and Northumberland presbyteries; and two Presbyterian homes.

Prayer

God of all hungry hearts, help churches never to be afraid to get closer to people in need. Help us to trust that if we do what we can, you will do what we cannot, through Christ, the Bread of Life. Amen.

Let us join in prayer for:

Presbytery Staff
Rev. Dr. Bill Knudsen, executive presbyter
Elder Bob Shandry, stated clerk
Elder Peter Wallace, treasurer
Deacon Patty Beggs, administrative assistant, resource center coordinator

PC(USA) General Assembly Staff
Dennis Blum, GAMC
Michele Blum, PPC

Daily Lectionary
☼ Ps. 65, 147:1–11 ☾ Ps. 125, 91
Gen. 16:1–14
Heb. 9:15–28; John 5:19–29

Presbytery Staff
Elder Al DerMovsesian, acting general presbyter
Rev. Bruce Barstow, stated clerk
Elder Larry Davis, business administrator
Rev. Jeanne Radak, associate executive for congregational ministry
Rev. Bill Reinhold, associate executive for mission partnerships and urban ministry
Rev. Linda Robinson, associate executive for pastoral ministry
Rev. Bill Thompson, associate for visitation
Rev. Michelle Grunseich, resources and communication director
Rev. Schaunel Steinnagel, hunger action enabler
Andrea Cameron, accounting manager
Karen Bannister, accounting clerk
Luis Mercado, property manager and computer tech
Caroline Jeffrey, Kirkwood administrator
Cinthia Andujar, administrative assistant
Amy Ayres, administrative assistant
Crystal Peterkin, administrative assistant
Betsey Radcliffe, administrative assistant
Dannette Rivers, hospitality and reception

PC(USA) General Assembly Staff
Sharrie Bobrow, OGA
Margaret Hall Boone, GAMC
Karen Bosc, GAMC

Daily Lectionary
☼ Ps. 143, 147:12–20 ☾ Ps. 81, 116
Gen. 16:15—17:14
Heb. 10:1–10; John 5:30–47

The Presbytery of Philadelphia

Pennsylvania

In the spring of 2007 nine congregations of the Presbytery of Philadelphia stepped into the flowing waters of God's Spirit through the Partnership for Missional Church™, a process of discerning God's activity in their neighborhoods and ways they can join in God's mission.

Tom Wray and Ron Dawkins discuss the missional challenge for Trinity Church.

Each congregation in the cluster is committed to spending three years in discovering their partners in ministry, experimenting in ways of connecting to those partners, and developing a plan to reach out to them. First Presbyterian Church of Glenolden has found new partners through a neighborhood event that helps members of the armed forces. A traditional Presbyterian congregation and a Pentecostal independent congregation provide ministry for the youth of their urban neighborhood.

After the commitment to the partnership ends in 2010 for the first cluster of congregations, many of them plan to continue this exciting spiritual journey. In late 2008 thirteen congregations joined a second cluster, and new ministries and partnerships are emerging. A third cluster of congregations will begin in late 2010 or early 2011.

The Partnership for Missional Church™ is a partnership among Church Innovations, the Synod of the Trinity, the presbytery, and God's flowing Spirit that continues to be the driving force and focus as the twenty-two congregations discover where God is calling them to ministry and partnership.

The Presbytery of Philadelphia is 137 congregations with 38,438 members, 1 new church development, 4 immigrant faith communities, 4 community ministries, and 1 missional faith community. Presbyterian-related Kirkwood Camp and Arcadia University are within the presbytery's bounds.

Prayer
Gracious God, we give you thanks for the ministry of the congregations of the Presbytery of Philadelphia. Grant them the vision and strength that will lead them to the places where you are already in ministry. May their ministries flourish as lights in the darkness. Amen.

Pittsburgh Presbytery

Pennsylvania

First Presbyterian Church of Duquesne is in the third poorest community in the state, one beset by violence, gangs, drugs, and teenage pregnancy. As a positive alternative to violence, in 2007 four teenage girls—Courtney, Yolanda, Jasmine, and Britney—started a chocolate candy-making business. At Angel (Always Needing God's Everlasting Love) Treats the motto is "Making the World a Sweeter Place." The girls attach a Scripture verse to each package and pray for those receiving their candy. The girls received a Self-Development of People grant to purchase supplies, update the church kitchen, and provide five additional youth with their first job experience. As the Angel Treats girls' lives change, they are helping more young people in the process. When they speak to groups, the girls share how God is blessing them and others through this endeavor.

The Angel Treats' success inspires other youth.

Judith Slater

They are learning how to produce, package, ship, market, do accounting, and hire and supervise others. Most of all they are learning that the cycle of poverty can be broken. All of the girls have improved academically since starting this business, and as Courtney puts it, "I am more into school now that I can see the practical reasons for learning. God is blessing our lives through this business." The girls are also imagining more possibilities for their future. For more information, call First Presbyterian Church of Duquesne at (412) 469-0750.

Pittsburgh Presbytery's 148 churches, 8 new church developments, and Crestfield Camp and Conference Center serve 40,834 members. Pittsburgh Theological Seminary is within its bounds.

Prayer

Lord, thank you for helping us imagine a different future. Amen.

Let us join in prayer for:

Presbytery Staff
Rev. Dr. Doug Portz, acting pastor to presbytery
Rev. Judi Slater, associate pastor for small-size congregations
Rev. Jay Lewis, stated clerk
Rev. Betty Angelini, executive director of Crestfield Camp and Conference Center
Rev. Karen Battle, director of justice ministries and mission
Elder Sharon Stewart, director of disciplemaking and spiritual growth
Elder Jeff Walley, business administrator
Elder Vera White, director of new church development, stewardship, and committee on ministry
Dina Blackwell, coordinator of resource center ministries
Lana Dumrauf, administrative assistant
Suzanne McHenry, administrative assistant
Elder Cindy Miller, administrative assistant
Elder Evelyn Moulton, receptionist
Dorothy Winter, financial secretary
Sydney Winter, administrative assistant

Presbyterian Media Mission
Elder Gregg Hartung, executive director
Elder Tina Hartung, office manager

PC(USA) General Assembly Staff
Randy Bowman, GAMC
Nancy Boxman, BOP

Daily Lectionary
☼ Ps. 88, 148 ☾ Ps. 6, 20
Gen. 17:15–27
Heb. 10:11–25; John 6:1–15

The Presbytery of Redstone

Pennsylvania

For over sixty years Pine Springs Camp (PSC) has been giving adults and children vital encounters with Jesus Christ. Supported by the Presbytery of Redstone since 1948, PSC remains a powerful evangelical and missional tool, a big influence in the lives of its participants.

"Camp played such a huge part in my life and relationship with Christ. As I grew from a Mini-venture camper to Mountains to Missions as a teen, Pine Springs never failed to present me with new challenges to help me take my faith seriously, to decide for myself that I was a follower of Jesus, and to learn to put that faith into action," explains Cristin Owen, a long-time camper.

Pine Springs has increased its focus on mission outreach with Mission Ex, a new junior high camp that has a distinct mission emphasis. Campers attend

Mission Ex participants perform a variety of service projects in the Johnstown area.

with their youth group leaders and participate in service projects in local distressed communities. The camp has also reached out with a less expensive day camp option to familiarize its community with what Pine Springs has to offer.

Redstone's mission outreach extends across the United States to places that have been devastated by flooding. Redstone volunteers continue to help rebuild areas of the Gulf destroyed by Hurricane Katrina and help with cleanup after floods strike elsewhere. Redstone's world mission focus is a partnership with the Sudan Presbyterian Evangelical Church. Its mission of prayer and presence reaches across borders and binds together the brothers and sisters of Christ. The presbytery and its 80 churches with 15,684 members and its partners seek to communicate the word, carry on the work of Christ, and change the world.

Prayer

Gracious God, be present in our midst this day as we seek to follow where you lead us. Be present in our dealings with all of the persons we will encounter this day. Help us to seek your guidance as we work together to seek ways to make this world a better place for all of your people. Amen.

The Lord's Day

Minute for Mission

Austin Presbyterian Theological Seminary

Sunday Lectionary and Hymns

Jer. 1:4–10
Lord, When I Came Into This Life
PH 522
God of the Prophets!
HB 520

Ps. 71:1–6
PPCS 63

1 Cor. 13:1–13
Though I May Speak
PH 335

Luke 4:21–30
God of Compassion, in Mercy Befriend Us
PH 261, HB 122

"For you shall go to all to whom I send you, and you shall speak whatever I command you" (Jer. 1:7). Bold words to Jeremiah, and to the many women and men still called to ministry. These days, seminary students often graduate with such large debt they can only "speak" to the larger congregations that can afford to call them.

Molly and Jim Crawley of First Presbyterian Church, Norman, Oklahoma, thought that a good way to support ministry would be through a gift to Austin Presbyterian Theological Seminary in the form of a three-year annual scholarship to cover tuition, room and board, and books for a student's entire seminary education. "The idea of supporting a school that is sending graduates out to small and suburban churches seemed like a good idea to us," said James Crawley.

Jody Horton

Deb Schmidt immerses herself in the preparation for her vocation—minister of Word and Sacrament.

That "someone" happens to be middler student Deb Schmidt from the rural town of Winfield, Kansas. Schmidt's home church, First Presbyterian, has about 250 members, and Schmidt is only the second person from there to attend seminary—the first attended more than fifty years ago. Schmidt says that the number of small churches without pastors in Kansas was part of her motivation to attend seminary. She was thrilled to be selected for the Crawley Scholarship. "I had already made up my mind to come here, but the scholarship definitely confirmed that this was the path I was to follow," aid Schmidt. She enjoyed getting to know the Crawleys when they visited the campus her first semester. Schmidt affirms, "It seems to me that we are in ministry together for whatever it is that God has planned."

—Shannon Neufeld, former associate for public relations,
Austin Presbyterian Theological Seminary, Austin, Texas

Prayer

Thanks be to you, O God, for continually calling people who, like Jeremiah, go and speak and live what you command. And thanks be for all those who devote their energies and substance toward making their paths clear. Through Jesus Christ our Lord. Amen.

The Presbytery of Shenango

Pennsylvania

Building Tables, Rebuilding Lives" has become the catchphrase for the Western Pennsylvania Table Project, which seeks to encourage the love of woodworking while creating handcrafted dining tables for survivors of Hurricane Katrina.

Under the direction of Jim Moose, and with support from the churches of the Presbytery of Shenango and other denominations, the Table Project is a community effort that gathers woodworkers and school students of varying skill levels to help ease the pain of many displaced families as they start over—by welcoming them home. "A table offers a center to a home, a place for meals, playing cards, doing homework. In short, it's a place for a family to be a family," explains Moose. "It was humbling to realize that a group from Western Pennsylvania could reach across 1,100 miles and make a difference in the lives of complete strangers."

Jim Moose adds, "I'm in my fifties, and this is the first time in my life that I've been involved in something where I felt I was making a difference. This project encourages people to become part of something bigger than themselves."

Volunteers from the Western Pennsylvania Table Project pause for a photo with Cindy and her new table.

To date, over 500 tables have been built and sent to New Orleans and the Gulf Coast, and several hundred more are projected to be sent over the coming months. To read more about the Western Pennsylvania Table Project and learn how to participate, visit www.westernpatableproject.org.

The presbytery is composed of 13,905 members in 68 churches in Lawrence and Mercer counties. Grove City and Westminster colleges lie within its bounds, as does the New Wilmington Mission Conference, with which Shenango has a covenant relationship.

Daily Lectionary
☼ Ps. 62, 145 ☾ Ps. 73, 9
Gen. 19:1–17 (18–23) 24–29
Heb. 11:1–12; John 6:27–40

Prayer
Gracious God, we thank you for involving us in your unfolding story. Continue to challenge and transform us by presenting opportunities to serve others in your name. Amen.

Upper Ohio Valley Presbytery

Ohio, West Virginia

This is a promising presbytery, though the area it covers has undergone major economic decline. The steel and coal industries, once the backbone of Upper Ohio Valley Presbytery's communities, have shut down almost completely. Workers by the thousands are now without income. Some lost their homes and claimed bankruptcy; others moved away in the hope of finding better opportunities.

Upper Ohio Valley Presbytery's Evangelism Committee has been active in encouraging sessions in their evangelism programs.

Amid continuing crises, the congregations within the presbytery are persistently seeking ways to bring about hope, peace, and justice. Several congregations have committed themselves to a long-term designation of 10–20 percent of their budgets to their communities' growing needs. Other congregations are sharing their time and talents with mission organizations. Many are generously supplying outreach institutions with food, clothing, and free medical attention.

Evangelism, the sharing of Christ's good news and love, is among the top priorities of the presbytery. Side by side with other forms of ministries of outreach, evangelism is sharing the gospel while feeding the hungry and sheltering the homeless.

The presbytery is also committed to providing church leaders with ideas, workshops, counseling, and financial assistance to help churches and members of the community cope with these very trying times.

The Upper Ohio Valley Presbytery covets all prayers in the hope that its communities will recognize the bounty of God's blessings that still surround us.

Upper Ohio Valley Presbytery's 89 churches have 8,625 members.

Prayer

God of promise and fulfillment, you caused Christ to come to earth as our Redeemer and Giver of new life. With that life, and empowered by your Holy Spirit, we set out in service. In Christ's name. Amen.

Tuesday, February 2

Let us join in prayer for:

Presbytery Staff
Rev. Dr. Royce L. Browder, general presbyter
Rev. Tom Armstrong, stated clerk and associate general presbyter for COM
Rev. Dr. Larry Kline, associate general presbyter for congregational nurture
Patty Oleska, administrative assistant
Cathy Cipriani, resource center coordinator
Nicole Reid, editor of *The Connector*
Amanda Stewart, treasurer
Nancy DeStefano, Christian educator and youth coordinator

PC(USA) General Assembly Staff
Rochelle Brinkley , FDN
Kathy Brinkman, GAMC
Sherry Britton, GAMC

Daily Lectionary

☼ Ps. 12, 146 ☾ Ps. 36, 7
Gen. 21:1–21
Heb. 11:13–22; John 6:41–51

Washington Presbytery

Pennsylvania

"So, what are you going to do about it?" was the question Rose heard as she pondered and prayed about a discussion in her Presbyterian Women (PW) Bible study group at Laboratory Presbyterian Church (LPC) in Washington, Pennsylvania. That discussion had been about choices in life and giving birth. Some in the group voiced their concern for new mothers, especially teenage mothers. At the next meeting Rose presented an idea for a mission project: collect baby supplies and clothes to give to new, teenage mothers along with a card reminding them that God loves them, too. From that vision, "Love in a Basket" began as a mission outreach of the PW of Laboratory Presbyterian Church with two laundry baskets filled with supplies donated by twelve women.

Members of the LPC of Washington prepare baskets of supplies for newborns for their Love in a Basket ministry.

Love in a Basket shares God's love with new mothers who don't have a support network. The women in the group line baskets with blankets and fill them with supplies for newborns. Then they tuck an inspirational note into each basket to let the new mothers know that someone is praying for them. The baskets are delivered through local nonprofits and private referrals.

Out of a believer's heart, Love in a Basket has become an ecumenical project sharing God's love. Since November 2004 the outreach of Love in a Basket has more than quadrupled in donations and distributions through the support of church members and friends, the other congregations in Washington Presbytery, the Synod of the Trinity, and other organizations. In a four-year period 450 baskets were delivered to new mothers in need of them.

Washington Presbytery is home to 63 churches and 10,639 members, Presbyterian-related Waynesburg University, and Presbyterian SeniorCare.

Prayer
Gracious God, we thank you for the privilege and honor of being people sent with the good news of Jesus Christ. In partnerships forged between churches, help us to be a church that helps people grow in your transforming love. Amen.

The Presbytery of West Virginia

West Virginia Ministry of Advocacy and Workcamps, Inc. (WVMAW), a nonprofit disaster recovery organization, began as a response to consecutive floods in 2001 and 2002. In McDowell County WVMAW confirmed that 67 percent of wastewater was straight-piped into the rivers and streams. McDowell County citizens and interested agencies formed a coalition and initiated a study to find a solution. Geography and economics pose challenges to traditional sewage systems, so alternative systems needed to be considered.

In 2006, with funding from Presbyterian Disaster Assistance (PDA), a demonstration alternative system was installed in a Head Start and Community Center. On January 12, 2009, about sixty people gathered in Ashland to celebrate the groundbreaking of the first such community system. A septic tank effluent gravity collection system with constructed wetland treatment cells, this eco-friendly wastewater treatment system is a model for finding creative alternatives for specific needs.

A Notre Dame mission group works on a drainfield in Ashland.

WVMAW is involved in educational programs with students as well as volunteers from colleges and universities who come to the state to learn about social and economic challenges in Appalachia. The desire for justice is seeking to end the cycle of poverty. And the desire for justice is motivating the cleanup of the rivers and streams for the health of the community and for all forms of life throughout this beautiful region.

Out of the hearts of the believers in the Presbytery of West Virginia, the Synod of the Trinity, and PDA flow streams of clean, living water. The presbytery is home to Davis and Elkins College, Bluestone Conference Center, Davis Stuart Home, and 143 congregations with 12,399 members.

Prayer

Forgive us, Lord, when we take everyday things for granted and damage the landscape of your glorious creation. O Well of Living Water, we seek your wisdom and guidance so that we do not diminish this world that sustains our lives. Through Christ we pray. Amen.

Thursday, February 4

Let us join in prayer for:

Presbytery Staff
Gay Mothershed, executive presbyter
John Bolt, stated clerk
Lois Coffey, treasurer/financial administrator
Margaret Bolt, office administrator
Erica Panaro, administrative assistant
Sherri Walker, information services director
Carolyn Arbuckle, hunger action enabler
Susan Sharp Campbell, associate, educational ministry
Terry Cunningham, associate, older adult ministry
Mary Jane Knapp, quadrant ministry
Mark Miller, Bluestone director
Karen Robinson, resource center director
Peter Vial, associate, congregational development

PC(USA) General Assembly Staff
Keith Brooks, GAMC
Analise Brown, GAMC
Anita Brown, GAMC

Daily Lectionary
☼ Ps. 116, 147:12–20 ☾ Ps. 26, 130
Gen. 23:1–20
Heb. 11:32—12:2; John 6:60–71

Let us join in prayer for:

Partners/Ministries
Project for Christian-Muslim Relations in Africa (PROCMURA): **Rev. Dr. Johnson Mbillah**, general adviser, **Rev. Angele Dogbe Wilson**, women's coordinator • All Africa Conference of Churches: **Rev. Dr. André Karamaga**, general secretary, **Archbishop Valentine Mokiwa**, president

PC(USA) General Assembly Staff
Brian Brown, FDN
Rev. Jon Brown, GAMC

Africa

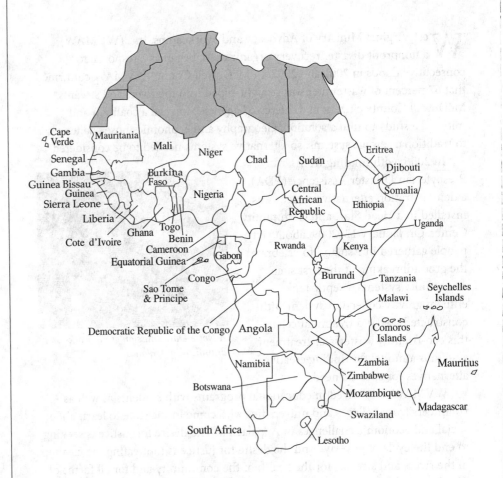

Daily Lectionary

☼ Ps. 84, 148 ☾ Ps. 25, 40
Gen. 24:1–27
Heb. 12:3–11; John 7:1–13

Africa

"Out of the believer's heart shall flow rivers of living water" (John 7:38).

Africa is blessed with rivers. The Nile, Congo, Zambezi, and Niger rivers are among the largest in the world. The basins that feed these rivers and others cover much of the whole continent. And yet over half of Africa's population, 300 million people, do not have access to safe, clean water to live healthy lives. This knowledge touches us deeply, as we know many of the people directly affected by these statistics. We walk closely with our church partners across Africa in programs designed to address this situation and many others.

Dr. Michael, the doctor in charge of Akobo Hospital (Sudan), discusses health work with Dr. Ingrid Reneau and Nancy McGaughey.

Reflecting on this verse I find myself thinking about another flow of living water that comes from a believer's heart, for we walk with our partners in a real way through the Presbyterian Church (U.S.A.) mission personnel who have answered God's call to mission. The love, care, gifts, and skills that flow from the many PC(USA) mission workers in Africa are amazing. If you are unfamiliar with them, you are missing a wonderful story of changed lives changing lives. At this time more than sixty long-term mission personnel are serving in Africa through the PC(USA), together with many more who are serving in various short-term capacities. I have the great joy of watching each of these people reach out in faith, called by God to go and share a love that surpasses all understanding. The need and calling remain, and today I am thrilled that our church has decided to reverse the trend toward sending fewer mission personnel. Perhaps you have felt God's call in your life, or know someone who is listening, and can take that step in faith that comes from a believing heart to pour forth rivers of living water. If so, we are anxious to talk with you.

Prayer

God of love, watch over the many people in Africa who do not have access to clean, safe water. Open our eyes to see your calling for us to have hearts that flow with rivers of living water. Show us and lead us in your will. Amen.

Let us join in prayer for:

Partners/Ministries
Christian Council of Liberia • Evangelical Church of the Republic of Niger:
Mr. Yahaya Cherif, general secretary, **Rev. Harouna Labo**, president, **Ibrahim Abdou**, permanent secretary • Evangelical Presbyterian Church of Togo: **Rev. Agbenoxeri Mawuli Awanyoh**, moderator, **Rev. Luther K. E. Degbovi**, synod secretary, **Mme. Caroline Abra Awu-Adzry Llahare**, presbytery executive • Botswana Christian Council: **David Modiega**, general secretary

PC(USA) General Assembly Staff
Sondra Brown, BOP
Trish Brown, OGA
Andrew Browne, BOP

Let us join in prayer for:

PC(USA) General Assembly Staff
Thomas Browne, GAMC
Rev. Vernon Broyles, OGA
Deborah Bruce, GAMC

Africa, *continued*

Jim McGill, along with his family, has been in mission service for many years in Malawi. Over time he has developed an expertise in water and sanitation that is sought in many other African contexts. His expertise comes from a knowledge of various water systems such as shallow wells or boreholes, but his real gift in ministry is the manner in which he engages people in the community in a way that brings them to own their own development, to know why they need clean water, and to have the means not only to get it but to keep it!

Ingrid Reneau, who is leading an important education ministry, is newer to mission service with the PC(USA). Working through the ecumenical ACROSS, Ingrid spends much of her time in very rural, marginalized southern Sudan training teachers how to teach. In a land where long ago school buildings were destroyed by war, she is building, person by person, new capacities for learning and growth with people who find new hope through the living waters flowing from Ingrid's heart.

Doug Tilton serves the PC(USA) in Africa as the Southern Africa regional liaison. In his work Doug crisscrosses the southern part of the continent, connecting with PC(USA) partners and members who come together in Christ's mission in that region. Regional liaisons serve in this important connecting role that enables us, as we go out in mission, to understand and learn cultural cues and dynamics. Working with our partners, regional liaisons help identify opportunities for long-term mission service in their region.

These are three examples of the many people and ways that the PC(USA) serves in mission in Africa. With each country page you will see the names of our mission personnel listed on the side column. Please be sure to pray for them, and look them up on the PC(USA) Web page to learn how better to pray for them.

—Elder Doug Welch, associate director, Mission Partners and Programs, General Assembly Mission Council

Daily Lectionary

☼ Ps. 63, 149 ☾ Ps. 125, 90
Gen. 24:28–38, 49–51
Heb. 12:12–29; John 7:14–36

Prayer

Lord, we lift before you the missionaries serving in Africa and beyond. Watch over them, and let them feel your presence in their lives in a real way today. Help them to be rivers of living water showing Christ's love to everyone they meet. In Christ's name. Amen.

The Lord's Day

Minute for Mission: Medical Benevolence Foundation

Sunday Lectionary and Hymns

Luke 5:1–11 tells the compelling story of Jesus preaching from Simon's fishing boat and then leading him to the greatest catch of fish he had ever had. In the work of the Medical Benevolence Foundation, we experience this same double joy in our short-term Mission Service Program. We proclaim the gospel in word and healing ministries, and we find our lives blessed in the work to which Jesus leads us.

Dr. Chip Lambert

Alanna (center) and other students learn about the healing ministry of Kikuyu Hospital.

Alanna Marie Grabouski is a pharmacy student who went on a Foundation trip to Kenya for medical students. She writes:

"The trip was a very good experience for me. Meeting and talking with the pharmacists allowed me to ask specific questions. I was discouraged by their obvious lack of space and computers and other problems, but I found myself thinking about ways they could be improved. This set a fire in me and made me realize how much I could help places like this in the future. Another huge experience for me was going out with the AIDS outreach clinic from Tumutumu. I had learned about the disease from facts and statistics, but meeting these people and learning about their lives and problems put a human face to it and ignited a desire in me to learn more about the disease. This trip made me realize that Christian mission service is working because of so many dedicated people. I don't know what form my support may take, but I do know that I want to tell people this good news and use my gifts to help."

—*Rev. Dr. Will Browne, executive director, Medical Benevolence Foundation*

Prayer

We thank you, God, that the service to which you call us gives us and those with whom we serve such joy and grace. Be with those most in need this day and make us instruments of your grace. In Jesus' name. Amen.

Isa. 6:1–8 (9–13)
Holy God, We Praise Your Name
PH 460
Holy! Holy! Holy! Lord God Almighty!
PH 138, HB 11

Ps. 138
I Will Give Thanks with My Whole Heart
PH 247

1 Cor. 15:1–11
This Is the Good News
PH 598

Luke 5:1–11
Tú Has Venido a la Orilla
(Lord, You Have Come to the Lakeshore)
PH 377

Daily Lectionary
☼ Ps. 103, 150 ☾ Ps. 117, 139
Gen. 24:50–67
2 Tim. 2:14–21; Mark 10:13–22

Let us join in prayer for:

PC(USA) People in Mission
Rev. Joshua Heikkila, regional liaison,
West Africa, World Mission

PC(USA) General Assembly Staff
Laura Bryan, OGA
Nikki Bryant, BOP
Elder Rob Bullock, GAMC

Ghana

Ghana is one of the most stable and prosperous democracies in Africa. Following a highly contested runoff election, a peaceful transfer of power from one political party to an opposition party took place early in January 2009—the second such transfer of political power in Ghana since the country was opened to multiparty democracy in 1992.

Ghanaian churches play a very critical role in developing and sustaining education at all levels throughout the country. The Evangelical Presbyterian Church, Ghana, recently spearheaded the establishment of the University of

Over 130 students are now attending the new University of the Volta Region.

the Volta Region in the region's capital city, Ho, thus bringing quality higher education to this rural and less developed area of Ghana. Its initial curriculum focuses on agribusiness, business management, marketing, pastoral ministry, and church management. Many of its instructors are retired professionals from the church, the business community, the educational community, and the government. Short-term volunteers from abroad are being sought to contribute their expertise to the development of the university's courses and programs. The vision is that this new university will faithfully serve the people of the Volta Region as it develops into a mature university.

—*John and Joyce Petro, members, Ghana Mission Network*

Total area: 92,456 sq. mi. (slightly smaller than Oregon). **Population:** 23,832,495. **Languages:** Asante, Ewe, other, English (official). **GDP per capita:** $1,500. **Literacy:** 57.9% (male 66.4%, female 49.8%). **Religions:** Christian, Muslim, traditional, other. **Life expectancy:** 59.85 years. **Human Development Index rank:** 142

Prayer

We pray, loving God, that your people in the Presbyterian Church of Ghana and the Evangelical Presbyterian Church, Ghana, will continue to follow the admonitions of the prophet Micah—to do justice, to love kindness, and to walk humbly with you, their God. Amen.

Ghana

Presbyterians engaged in mission relationships with partners in Ghana gather regularly to support and learn from each other through the Ghana Mission Network. The network includes presbyteries with Ghana partnerships, as well as congregations, organizations, and individuals engaged in mission in Ghana. The PC(USA)'s two partner denominations in Ghana provide regular representation to ensure that network members coordinate their mission strategies and that they receive guidance on cultural and logistical issues. The association of Presbyterian immigrant congregations in the United States also provides valuable guidance and resources for the network.

Rev. Alice Ankutse, pastor of the Sokode District of the Evangelical Presbyterian Church, Ghana, enjoys singing at a Ghana Mission Network partnership meeting.

Glen Hallead

The network sponsored a partnership meeting in Ghana. Sixty delegates, twenty each from the PC(USA), the Presbyterian Church of Ghana, and the Evangelical Presbyterian Church, Ghana, met for four days of worship, fellowship, and discussion. They considered men's and women's issues, topics including HIV/AIDS and other medical issues, education, domestic violence and family issues, building construction, ministry to orphans and other vulnerable society members, leadership development, relations with Muslims and traditional religionists, and development projects. Insights from this meeting continue to guide the relationships and activities of network members in Ghana.

—*Rev. Peter C. de Vries, Mars, Pennsylvania; convener, Ghana Mission Network*

Prayer

Lord God, in your good pleasure you have invited us to share in your work in creation, not because you need our efforts, but because you love us. Guide the relationships that you have formed between your children in the United States and in Ghana so that they may know the joy of a life shared in your grace. Amen.

Partners/Ministries
Presbyterian Church of Ghana (PCG): **Rev. Dr. Yaw Frimpong-Manso**, moderator, **Rev. Herbert Opong**, clerk of General Assembly • Evangelical Presbyterian Church, Ghana (EPCG): **Rev. Francis Amenu**, moderator, **Rev. Godwin Kwaku Osiakwa**, synod clerk, **Mrs. Lydia Adajawah**, presbyter executive • Christian Council of Ghana • Presbytery Partnerships: Presbytery of Lake Michigan with the EPCG; Presbytery of Greater Atlanta, Foothills Presbytery, Presbytery of the James, Presbytery of Lackawanna, Presbytery of Mid-Kentucky, Presbytery of New Brunswick, Salem Presbytery, Presbytery of Denver, Presbytery of Chicago, and Presbytery of Milwaukee with the PCG

PC(USA) General Assembly Staff
Cherrle Burch, FDN
Pamela Burdine, GAMC
Janie Burton, OGA

Daily Lectionary

☼ Ps. 42, 146 ☾ Ps. 102, 133
Gen. 26:1–6, 12–33
Heb. 13:17–25; John 7:53—8:11

Let us join in prayer for:

Partners/Ministries
Presbyterian Church of Nigeria: **Rev. U. B. Usung**, moderator, **Rev. Ndukwe Nwachukwa**, principal clerk • Christian Council of Nigeria

PC(USA) General Assembly Staff
Janet Bushick, BOP
Marisa Bustamante, GAMC

Nigeria

The women of the Presbyterian Church of Nigeria (PCN) continue to lead their denomination and country in outreach to their communities. In several places the women have formed nongovernmental organizations (NGOs) to help respond to human need. Presbyterian Reach-Out Mission (PROM) is one such NGO that provides educational assistance and care for widows and orphans, and works to empower women. The Yaba Parish in Lagos assists women to access microfinance loans for their small businesses, and patronage has been high. Women of the Hope Waddell Parish of the PCN have an NGO called HOWAD Women. Its main concern is addressing HIV/AIDS issues through educational activities for women and peer educators programs.

Northern Calabar women built stores that they rented out to PCN women. They also have embarked on such skill training as hat and bead making to enable women to support their families. PCN women in northern Nigeria are organizing a Muslim/Christian dialogue toward actualizing peace in the troubled area for women irrespective of religion. Women in the Mary Slessor Parish have an active welfare department for care of widows and the elderly and each month support a center with food items and toiletries for physically challenged persons. The ministers' wives within the Calabar Synod have registered an NGO called Golden Vessels to handle advocacy issues with the government and have a proposal for a guest house for which they are seeking funds. At the national level, women of the Presbyterian Church of Nigeria organized an International Women's Triennial Conference in September 2008. Women from Canada, Ghana, Kenya, the United States, and elsewhere joined more than 5,000 women of the PCN.

—*Women of the Presbyterian Church of Nigeria*

Total area: 356,669 sq. mi. (slightly more than twice the size of California). **Population:** 149,299,090. **Languages:** English (official), Hausa, Yoruba, Igbo, Fulani. **GDP per capita:** $2,300. **Literacy:** 68% (male 75.7%, female 60.6%). **Religions:** Muslim, Christian, indigenous beliefs. **Life expectancy:** 46.94 years. **Human Development Index rank:** 154.

Prayer

Dear Lord, we are thrilled by the great energy that the women in Nigeria have for your mission. We lift up to you the economic empowerment activities for women and educational assistance for children of the poor. We pray for women in church leadership positions. Give strength and wisdom to the women who seek to raise funds for their many projects from women who are poor. In Christ's name. Amen.

Daily Lectionary
☼ Ps. 89:1–18, 147:1–11 ☾ Ps. 1, 33
Gen. 27:1–29
Rom. 12:1–8; John 8:12–20

Cameroon

I first met Joseph Zombo when he was a mathematics teacher at College Johnston. Quiet natured, Joseph is always trying to learn more for the service of the Presbyterian Church in Cameroon. Completing his seminary training at a time when his church was polarized and on the verge of splitting, Joseph calmly tried to stick to his work in support of the education ministries of the church. Despite having almost no computer training, he has taught himself and built databases and spreadsheets to help the church manage its personnel and finances.

Joseph Zombo teaches at a seminar for administrators of Presbyterian schools.

Spreadsheets and databases may not seem that noteworthy in the context of missions, but many ministries struggle because of an inability or unwillingness to manage and use resources in ways that help ministries flourish. The Rev. Zombo has both the capacity and the spirit to help his church. To counter jealousies and conflict between pastors in poor rural congregations and those in large urban congregations, he helps his presbytery manage a fund that ensures every pastor will receive a base salary. This fund also supports retired pastors and widows. Now that Joseph has fallen ill and become partially paralyzed, his church and the presbytery try to accommodate his limitations. In recognition of the value of his work, the presbytery plans to train others to operate and maintain the computer system he has developed, thus ensuring the continuity of the presbytery fund.

—*Jeff Boyd, PC(USA) regional liaison, Central Africa*

Total area: 183,568 sq. mi. (slightly larger than California). **Population:** 18,879,301. **Languages:** 24 major African language groups, English and French (official). **GDP per capita:** $2,300. **Literacy:** 67.9% (male 77%, female 59.8%). **Religions:** indigenous beliefs, Christian, Muslim. **Life expectancy:** 53.69 years. **Human Development Index rank:** 150.

Prayer

Faithful God, thank you for your servants like Joseph Zombo who share from their heart, mind, and soul to build up your church and its ministries. Amen.

Let us join in prayer for:

PC(USA) People in Mission
World Mission: **Jeffrey Boyd**, regional liaison, Central Africa, **Christi Boyd**, Joining Hands companionship facilitator • Presbyterian Church in Cameroon: **Rev. Shirley Hill**, public health worker, HIV/AIDS, **Rev. Leisa Wagstaff**, professor, Presbyterian Teacher Training College, Mbengwi

PC(USA) General Assembly Staff
Essie Buxton, GAMC
Kelly Cahill, BOP
Joyce Campbell, GAMC

Daily Lectionary
☼ Ps. 97, 147:12–20 ☾ Ps. 16, 62
Gen. 27:30–45
Rom. 12:9–21; John 8:21–32

Let us join in prayer for:

Partners/Ministries
Presbyterian Church in Cameroon •
Eglise Presbyterienne Camerounaise:
Rev. Dr. Dieudonne Massi Gams, general
secretary • Council for Protestant Churches
in Cameroon (CEPCA): **Rev. Dr. Jean-
Emile Ngue**, general secretary • Network
Fighting Hunger in Cameroon (RELUFA):
Valéry Nodem, national coordinator •
Presbytery Partnerships with Cameroon:
Presbytery of Chicago and Presbytery of the
Twin Cities Area with Joining Hands
Against Hunger

PC(USA) General Assembly Staff
Rev. Dr. Jerry Cannon, GAMC
Kate Cannon, GAMC
Suzan Cantrell, GAMC

Cameroon, *continued*

Cameroon was among the first countries in which the denomination initiated Joining Hands Against Hunger. Supported by One Great Hour of Sharing, this mission program enables Presbyterians in the United States and anti-hunger networks of churches, nonprofit organizations, and grassroots groups overseas to engage with each other in a holistic, international hunger ministry.

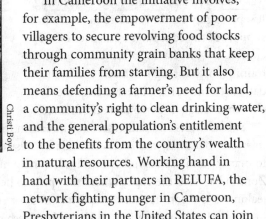

Jeanne Nouah, spokesperson for the indigenous Bagyeli tribe, shares about the impact of an oil project on her people.

In Cameroon the initiative involves, for example, the empowerment of poor villagers to secure revolving food stocks through community grain banks that keep their families from starving. But it also means defending a farmer's need for land, a community's right to clean drinking water, and the general population's entitlement to the benefits from the country's wealth in natural resources. Working hand in hand with their partners in RELUFA, the network fighting hunger in Cameroon, Presbyterians in the United States can join in as companions, breaking bread with one another as an expression of the communal nature of the church's global hunger strategy.

Christ intertwines water and bread as metaphors for the physical and spiritual dimensions of his ministries. They flow into each other and become an inseparable stream to express a quality of life that supersedes worldly needs and desires. For this godly realm, compassionate love, responsible stewardship, and moral justice join into a wholesome discipleship. Converging at the heart of this missional church, Presbyterians together can form an unstoppable flow of life-giving water.

—*Christi Boyd, PC(USA) mission co-worker*

Daily Lectionary
☼ Ps. 51, 148 ☾ Ps. 142, 65
Gen. 27:46—28:4, 10–22
Rom. 13:1–14; John 8:33–47

Prayer
Permeate us all with your Spirit, God, so the heart of our church bursts into rivers of living water, joining up with those flowing from the hearts of believers around the globe, and flood this world to bring forth life the way you intend it to be. Amen.

Equatorial Guinea

It was the dry season in Equatorial Guinea and the days of March were hot. I was riding a bus from the city of Bata to the city of Ebibeyin, visiting congregations. When the bus came to a stop we observed a large group of people with plastic containers. They were lining up to get water from a fresh spring to take back home. They were willing to walk a great distance and stand in a long line because they had no other source of drinking water.

Viewing this scene made me realize how many times the church has left its living source and secure foundation of life—Jesus Christ. Christians, even some leaders, sometimes disregard God's love and compassion and the servant nature of Christian ministry.

—Andres Garcia, PC(USA) mission co-worker

Total area: 10,831 sq. mi. (slightly smaller than Maryland). **Population:** 633,441. **Languages:** Spanish and French (official), Fang, Bubi. **GDP per capita:** $31,400. **Literacy:** 87% (male 93.4%, female 80.5%). **Religions:** nominally Christian and predominantly Roman Catholic, pagan practices. **Life expectancy:** 61.61 years. **Human Development Index rank:** 115.

Rwanda

Rwanda is a beautiful, green land of a thousand hills in the Great Lakes region of Africa. It is also a predominantly Christian country. Since the 1994 genocide the Rwandan people have taken many strides toward unity, and the churches have worked hard at ecumenism. They have sought to aid the orphans and widows of the war and to help those still traumatized by its brutality. The PC(USA) over the last two decades has maintained a partnership relationship with the Presbyterian Church in Rwanda. It has also given scholarships to students at the Protestant Theological College of Butare, a nondenominational seminary that is educating church leaders for a new era.

—Michael Parker, PC(USA) coordinator, International Evangelism,
General Assembly Mission Council

Total area: 10,169 sq. mi. (slightly smaller than Maryland). **Population:** 10,473,282. **Languages:** Kinyarwanda (official), French (official), English (official), Kiswahili. **GDP per capita:** $900. **Literacy:** 70.4% (male 76.3%, female 64.7%). **Religions:** Roman Catholic, Protestant, Adventist, Muslim, other. **Life expectancy:** 50.52 years. **Human Development Index rank:** 165.

Prayer

God of the Word and the world, grant the church some new Nehemiahs so it will be able to reencounter the fresh living water of the gospel of Jesus Christ. Amen.

Let us join in prayer for:

PC(USA) People in Mission
Reformed Presbyterian Church of Equatorial Guinea (IRPGE): **Andres Garcia**, evangelist/church administrator, **Gloria Garcia Salazar**, evangelist/church administrator

Partners/Ministries
IRPGE: **Rev. Manuel Nzoh Asumu**, general secretary • Presbyterian Church in Rwanda (EPR): **Dr. Elisee Musemakweli**, president • Christian Council of Rwanda: **Rev. Emmanuel Nkusi**, general secretary • Presbytery Partnership with Rwanda: Presbytery of Kiskiminetas with the EPR

PC(USA) General Assembly Staff
Christine Cappo, BOP
Rev. Timothy Cargal, OGA

Daily Lectionary
☼ Ps. 104, 149 ☾ Ps. 138, 98
Gen. 29:1–20
Rom. 14:1–23; John 8:47–59

The Lord's Day

Minute for Mission: Transfiguration of the Lord

Music is a big part of ministry in my church, Hopewell Presbyterian, in Louisville, Kentucky. Our choirs, praise band, and congregational hymn singing add meaning and depth to our weekly worship.

On special occasions like holidays, our adult chancel choir hits the road to perform in several local nursing homes. I've often heard my pastor, the Rev. Tom Dillard, and other choir members remark on what an "awesome experience" it is to participate in this form of ministry to some of our most vulnerable and fragile brothers and sisters. It is truly a blessing to see the looks on the faces of the residents as the music flows over them. Doubt and fear and loneliness begin to subside and are replaced by beaming smiles and sparkling eyes.

I was blessed enough to witness this very tangible reminder of God's love flowing through us in late April 2009. In the final stages of terminal cancer, my dad, Paul, mentioned to Tom when he stopped by for a visit how his physical condition prevented him from attending worship and how terribly he missed hearing the music. So, on a warm and beautiful Sunday afternoon, my pastor and a dozen or so choir members and friends drove to my parents' house to spend time in prayer and song.

Sitting on the front porch steps next to my dad in his wheelchair, I could see the transformative power this visit had on him, how calm and peaceful he became as familiar hymns sung a cappella surrounded him. Just as Moses' face shone as he descended Mt. Sinai after talking with God, so too, did my dad's face begin to reflect the comfort of God's presence.

As we celebrate Transfiguration of the Lord Sunday, it is good to reflect on what gifts and talents God has blessed each of us with, and how we might use them to bring God's love to others.

—*Elder Donald J. Cecil, advertising manager*, Presbyterians Today,
General Assembly Mission Council

Prayer

Dear God, we give thanks for your gift of beloved Jesus. Just as he was transformed on the mountaintop, guide us and help us to use our gifts and talents wisely to transform the hearts of others and make them your servants and our brothers and sisters in Christ. Amen.

Sudan

RECONCILE is a Christian organization created by the New Sudan Council of Churches to provide training in peace building through civic education, trauma healing, and conflict transformation. In February 2009 we opened the RECONCILE Peace Institute (RPI), which offers three-month certificate courses in community-based trauma healing and in peace studies and conflict transformation.

Evangelist Peter Mama (here with his wife and child) learned how to minister more effectively in his community through a course offered by RECONCILE.

One of the participants is Presbyterian Church of Sudan (PCOS) evangelist Peter Mama, a paraplegic. Peter serves a PCOS Murle congregation. He was a refugee in Ethiopia when the government fell and the Ethiopian army chased all refugees out of the country. When everyone else ran for their lives, they left Peter behind. For twenty-seven days Peter crawled on his hands and searched for food and water until he reached Pochalla, Sudan. Through his ordeal Peter held on to his faith, repeating to himself, "God is greater than everything in the world. If it weren't for God I would be dead. I will follow Christ until I die." Peter's resilience and deep faith in Christ are inspirations to us all. We are delighted to be able to help him improve his skills to minister more effectively to his community.

—Debbie Braaksma, PC(USA) mission co-worker

Total area: 967,499 sq. mi. (slightly more than one-quarter the size of the United States). **Population:** 41,087,825. **Languages:** Arabic (official), English (official), Nubian, Ta Bedawie, diverse dialects of Nilotic, Nilo-Hamitic, Sudanic languages. **GDP per capita:** $2,200. **Literacy:** 61.1% (male 71.8%, female 50.5%). **Religions:** Sunni Muslim, indigenous beliefs, Christian. **Life expectancy:** 51.42 years. **Human Development Index rank:** 146.

Prayer

Heavenly Father, we thank you for your promise to be especially near to the brokenhearted. Please empower RECONCILE to be an agent of peace and healing in this war-torn land, and continue to bless its ministry. In the name of the Prince of Peace. Amen.

Monday, February 15

Let us join in prayer for:

PC(USA) People in Mission ACROSS: **Nancy McGaughey**, health coordinator, **Dr. Ingrid Reneau**, education officer • **Rev. Debra Blane**, theology lecturer, Nile Theological College • Resource Centre for Civil Leadership (RECONCILE): **Rev. Debra Braaksma**, program and project management officer, **Delvin Braaksma**, program and project management officer

PC(USA) General Assembly Staff **Jackie Carter**, GAMC **Sylvia Carter**, GAMC **Toni Carver-Smith**, GAMC

Daily Lectionary
☼ Ps. 5, 145 ☾ Ps. 82, 29
Prov. 27:1–6, 10–12
Phil. 2:1–13; John 18:15–18, 25–27

Let us join in prayer for:

Partners/Ministries
Presbyterian Church of Sudan (PCOS):
Rev. Peter Makuac Nyak, moderator,
Rev. Paul Bol Kuel, vice moderator,
Rev. Gideon Tai Tudeal, general secretary,
Rev. James Apay Ochalla, general
treasurer • Sudan Presbyterian Evangelical
Church (SPEC): **Rev. James Par Tap**,
moderator, **Rev. Simon Koak Bol**,
assistant moderator, **Ismail Kanani**,
general secretary, **Rev. Yohanan Ali Kuku**,
secretary deputy • Nile Theological College:
Rev. Thomas Maluit, principal • ACROSS:
Rev. Bernard Suwa • Resource Centre for
Civil Leadership (RECONCILE) • Sudan
Council of Churches: **Rev. Peter Tibi**,
general secretary • Presbytery Partnerships:
Trinity Presbytery with the PCOS;
Presbytery of Redstone and Presbytery
of Shenango with the SPEC

PC(USA) General Assembly Staff
Debbie Cassady, PILP
Molly Casteel, OGA

Daily Lectionary
☼ Ps. 42, 146 ☾ Ps. 102, 133
Prov. 30:1–4, 24–33
Phil. 3:1–11; John 18:28–38

Sudan, *continued*

I n the Nuba Mountains of Sudan is a brand new Bible school. There more than twenty young evangelists are being educated in both Arabic and English to reach out into the African bush with the good news of Jesus Christ. Students at the Kumo Bible School walk for hours every week to get to places where they have established preaching centers—similar to what we in the PC(USA) call new church development sites. Each student builds a one-room dwelling made of mud brick with a thatched roof, which will be his dormitory space while studying at Kumo. A small, two-room classroom building was constructed with a grant from a woman in the Presbytery of Shenango, and two motorbikes were purchased with gifts of money from the Presbytery of Redstone.

Women sew on treadle machines provided by the PW of the Synod of the Trinity.

Elizabeth Ajak of the Doleib Hill Presbytery of the Presbyterian Church of Sudan met with the coordinating team (CT) of Presbyterian Women (PW) in the Synod of the Trinity. Elizabeth spoke passionately about the need to make microcredit loans available to women so they can learn skills and provide for their families. There was no money available in the budget for such a request, so the members of the CT decided to make personal contributions and invite their PW groups to contribute to a fund that would be taken to Sudan several months later. The $6,000 that was raised was used to purchase sewing machines and other equipment, and training is now available so that women can become entrepreneurs. This is the gift that keeps on giving because the loans are repaid, and equipment and training are again made available to other women.

—*Sylvia Carlson, chair, the Presbytery of Redstone Mission Committee*

Prayer
God of grace and truth, we give you thanks for the gift of life and for the beauty of your creation. As we pray, we ask your presence among the many peoples of Sudan as they seek to provide for their families and to discover the ways that lead to peace. We pray these things in the name and for the sake of Jesus Christ, our Lord. Amen.

Ash Wednesday

Minute for Mission

An old Latin adage says: "It's as useless as pouring water into a sieve." Imagine the sight of that—endlessly trying to fill up a container covered with holes!

If we're not careful, our spiritual lives can easily wind up just like that. Without realizing it, we fall into bad patterns, and before long, they control and define us, stifling our hope, blocking our spiritual potential. We may waste days and even weeks moaning that God can never love us, that we can never change.

But that's simply not true! In fact, that's precisely why hope is a virtue. When we insist on pouring the water of our precious lives through the sieve of hopelessness, we're wasting it. We give in to despair, rather than let the love of God draw us into hope.

Today we begin the holy season of Lent, a time of self-examination, a time when Christians are challenged to make changes in their lives as they remember the passion of Jesus Christ. The heart and soul of Lent is to admit our failings humbly, to seek God's forgiveness, and to make a fresh start.

We have a choice. We can go on with life as usual, continuing in our unhelpful patterns and believing the lie that there's not a thing we can do about our weaknesses and shortcomings—in other words, pour water into our sieve. Or we can, with God's help, make a fresh start.

The ashes we receive today are a stark reminder that we will someday die and return to dust. They remind us that we have a limited time in which to act—to make a choice about how we want to live.

So, day by day in this Lenten season, rely on God for assistance, and with a loving and peaceful heart, honor your commitment to change as you await the coming of Easter.

—Rev. Jeffrey Lawrence, publisher, Presbyterians Today,
General Assembly Mission Council

Prayer

Good and gracious Lord, in your great love you ask us to return to you with our whole heart, with fasting and weeping and mourning. Show us the way to repentance and forgiveness. Increase our hope. Change our hearts. Guide us through this holy season of Lent, and show us the joy of the Resurrection. In Jesus' name we pray. Amen.

Let us join in prayer for:

PC(USA) General Assembly Staff
Sharon Castillo, BOP
Rhonda Cates, BOP
Nancy Cavalcante, GAMC

Daily Lectionary
☉ Ps. 5, 147:1–11 ☾ Ps. 27, 51
Amos 5:6–15
Heb. 12:1–14; Luke 18:9–14

Daily Lectionary
☼ Ps. 27, 147:12–20 ☾ Ps. 126, 102
Hab. 3:1–10 (11–15) 16–18
Phil. 3:12–21; John 17:1–8

Ethiopia

A young resident of Gilo can again attend school.

Southwest of Gambella, near Ethiopia's border with Sudan, the lowlands become absolutely flat. Occasional trees break up the sea of eight-foot-tall grass. During the rainy season the whole area is a vast swamp, and during the dry season dust hangs suspended in the humid air, turning sunsets orange and red and brown. Whirlwinds form ominous pillars, visible either as white with dust or black with ash, where cattle herders have burned off the grass to promote fresh growth.

Gilo, a very isolated Presbyterian school, was closed for two years because of violence that culminated in 2003. Ethnic tensions flared between the Nuer and the Anuak, complicated by 380,000 Sudanese refugees, rebel incursions, and military reprisals. Thousands of people were killed, and tens of thousands fled the area. Soldiers used the school's murals of the human body and the solar system as target practice. The well was vandalized and filled with rock and scrap metal. All large animals, including elephants and giraffes, were slaughtered to feed the roving armies.

But the school has been reopened by the local church. The walls are still pockmarked and the well still useless, but from the efforts of dedicated teachers new hope flows. They teach up to 117 children in each stifling classroom or alternate classes outside under the tattered trees. They teach music by making lutes from cooking oil tins from the UN refugee camps. They teach art by having students sculpt lumpy giraffes and elephants from mud. In this hostile place they embody the power of God's undying love.

—*Bruce Whearty, former PC(USA) mission co-worker*

Total area: 435,186 sq. mi. (slightly less than twice the size of Texas). **Population:** 85,237,338. **Languages:** Amarigna, Oromigna, Tigrigna, Somaligna, other local languages, English. **GDP per capita:** $800. **Literacy:** 42.7% (male 50.3%, female 35.1%). **Religions:** Christian, Muslim, traditional, other. **Life expectancy:** 55.41 years. **Human Development Index rank:** 169.

Prayer
God of hope, even when we are surrounded by whirlwinds and destruction, help us bear witness to your joy and love. Amen.

Ethiopia

In February 2009 the Ethiopian Evangelical Church Mekane Yesus (EECMY) held a Jubilee celebration. It was the 50th anniversary of the constituting of the EECMY as a national church body and the 110th anniversary of the proclamation of the gospel in the west of Ethiopia, which began with the Swedish Evangelical Mission.

Ann Reimer, Breezy Lusted, Didumo and Pastor Akway Ochudha, and Niles Reimer participate in the Jubilee celebration.

PC(USA) mission volunteer Marie (Breezy) Lusted writes that the Anuak Bible translation work continues to progress toward completion. There are a number of the books of the Bible that await final review by the Bible Society's consultant, but the translation team is hopeful that by the end of 2009 the whole Bible will be ready to submit to the Bible Society of Ethiopia for publishing.

Mission co-workers John and Gwen Haspels praise God that the Suri Project began 2009 in the black despite rising costs and declining income. Churches have written to John and Gwen that they are cutting their budgets, and at the national level giving has fallen. They write, "We are excited, however, to see that God is not limited by our limitations. God is doing a new work among the Suri by drawing them to himself through faith in Jesus Christ. There have been more than 130 baptisms in the last few months. We are witnessing an outpouring of the Holy Spirit on the Suri church where young people cannot seem to get enough of God and spend hours in his presence each day. What is interesting to us is that God is revealing himself to them as 'Baba,' Father. As this happens, the hearts of the Suri fathers are becoming more responsive to their own children. Praise God!"

Prayer

Dear God, thank you for the witness and ministry of the EECMY, for the outpouring of your Spirit among the Suri, and for the birthing of the Anuak translation of the Bible. We ask that you would continue to guide and bless these ministries. In Jesus' name. Amen.

Let us join in prayer for:

Partners/Ministries
Ethiopian Evangelical Church Mekane Yesus (EECMY): **Rev. Dr. Wakeseyoum Idossa**, president, **Rev. Dereje Jemberu**, vice president, **Mr. Almaw Gari**, treasurer • Illubabor Bethel Synod: **Rev. Yadeta Kirita**, president • Eastern Gambella Bethel Synod: **Ato Adak Ujulu**, president • Southwest Bethel Synod: **Rev. Petros Tsanu**, president • Western Gambella Bethel Synod: **Qes Ding Gach**, president • Western Wollega Bethel Synod: **Rev. Worati Galacha**, president • Bethel Mekane Yesus School: **Rev. Teferi Teressa**, director • Ethiopian Graduate School of Theology: **Dr. Desta Heliso**, president • Bethel Synod Coordination Office: **Rev. Teferi Berkessa**, coordinator • Bethel Evangelical Secondary School: **Mr. Abebe Muse**, director • Berhane Yesus Elementary School: **Mr. Amanuel Tesfaye**, director • Presbytery Partnerships: Presbytery of Shenandoah, Presbytery of Susquehanna Valley, and Washington Presbytery with the EECMY

PC(USA) General Assembly Staff
Elder Perry Chang, GAMC
Rev. Jon Chapman, GAMC
Sandra Charles, GAMC

Daily Lectionary

☼ Ps. 22, 148 ☾ Ps. 105, 130
Ezek. 18:1–4, 25–32
Phil. 4:1–9; John 17:9–19

Daily Lectionary
☼ Ps. 43, 149 ☾ Ps. 31, 143
Ezek. 39:21–29
Phil. 4:10–20; John 17:20–26

Kenya

Pastor Johnson Wambua was in class at the Nairobi International School of Theology (NIST) when he received news that his church had been burned to the ground in the January 2008 post-election violence. He rushed back to find only ashes where the church once stood, though miraculously a small school run by the church was still standing. By the time Kenya stabilized, most of Pastor Wambua's five hundred church members had fled or been displaced. But the school was intact, and there he began to rebuild his congregation.

One year later, a new congregation had emerged with more than five hundred new members. How did God do it? Wambua beamed as he talked about how his fellow students collected food and clothing to be distributed to

families in need in the area. His strategy was to give items of adult clothing to the children at the school, who then took them home to their parents and older siblings. He and a few others later visited their homes to see what other needs they had. Touched by the concern, the families began coming for Sunday worship.

Pastor Johnson Wambua shares updates about his ministry with Dr. Peter Kariuki, dean of students at the NIST.

Convinced of the strategic role of children in ministry, the church began outreach among the community's children. At a recent special event, of the 110 children who attended seventy gave their lives to Christ that day, and they are now bringing along their friends and families. Through a soft-spoken pastor God is growing the church and transforming a community. Out of fires of destruction flows living water.

—*Marta Bennett, PC(USA) mission co-worker*

Total area: 224,962 sq. mi. (slightly more than twice the size of Nevada). **Population:** 39,002,772. **Languages:** English and Kiswahili (official), indigenous languages. **GDP per capita:** $1,600. **Literacy:** 85.1% (male 90.6%, female 79.7%). **Religions:** Protestant, Roman Catholic, indigenous beliefs, Muslim, other. **Life expectancy:** 57.86 years. **Human Development Index rank:** 144.

Prayer
Loving God, though terrible trials may seem overwhelming, you are the source of new life, working through those who are faithful. Help us each to be faithful, wherever we are. Amen.

The Lord's Day

Minute for Mission: Self-Development of People

For most of us when we need water, we turn on the faucet and safe, clean water gushes forth. Imagine, then, living where all your water must be carried to your home from a distance, either on your back or in a wheelbarrow or donkey-pulled cart. This is the situation that the people of Mbuuni Village in Machakos, Kenya, experienced every day.

Families of Mbuuni Village now have access to clean water because of their partnership with SDOP.

The hundred families of Mbuuni Village approached the Presbyterian Committee on Self-Development of People (SDOP), requesting and receiving financial help to build a cement water tank that would catch, hold, and distribute rain water. The lives of the villagers have been permanently changed because Presbyterians, through One Great Hour of Sharing, helped to bring safe, clean water to Mbuuni Village.

Self-Development of People funds community groups of disadvantaged and underprivileged people in the United States and around the world. Presbyterians can help community groups in need by sharing information with them about the SDOP program. To be funded by SDOP, a community group must be oppressed by poverty or social systems, and the individuals in the group must want to take charge of their own lives and be organized—or in the process of becoming organized—to do something about their situation. Their plan must be one that will produce long-term changes for their lives or communities. To be funded, groups must control their projects themselves and benefit directly from the work. More information is available on the Self-Development of People Web site at www.pcusa.org/sdop.

—Rev. Wayne Gnatuk, associate for church-wide relations, Self-Development of People, General Assembly Mission Council

Prayer

God of Shalom, in our affluence, keep us ever mindful of the poor here and around the world who are also your children and who thirst for clean, safe water. Through our prayers and through our generosity, may they be blessed. In the name of Jesus Christ. Amen.

Let us join in prayer for:

Partners/Ministries
Presbyterian Church of East Africa (PCEA):
Rev. David Riitho Gathanju, moderator,
Rev. Festus Gitonga, general secretary,
Rev. Francis Ndungu Njoroge, deputy
general secretary, **Mr. Johnson Njatha
Wathiri**, treasurer • Christian
Organizations Research Advisory Trust:
Margaret W. Mwaura, executive director •
Daystar University: **Rev. Dr. Godfrey
Nguru**, vice chancellor • National Council
of Churches of Kenya: **Rev. Mutava
Musyimi**, general secretary • Presbyterian
University of East Africa: **Prof. Kihumbu
Thairu**, vice chancellor, **Dr. Timothy
Henry Gatara**, deputy vice chancellor •
St. Paul's Theological College: **Dr. Timothy
Wachira**, vice chancellor • Presbytery
Partnerships: Presbytery of Blackhawk,
Cimarron Presbytery, Presbytery of Detroit,
Presbytery of John Knox, Presbytery of
Los Ranchos, National Capital Presbytery,
Presbytery of Newton, Presbytery of
Northern Plains, Presbytery of the
Redwoods, and Presbytery of West
Virginia with the PCEA

PC(USA) General Assembly Staff
Dorothy Clark, BOP
Martha Clark, GAMC

We wanted to write an upbeat letter from Kenya, to tell you wonderful stories that would lift your spirits and make your heart sing. But how can we sing when the poor around us are experiencing such utter despair?

Today we learned that hospitals have run out of the tuberculosis vaccine for children. We have a Kenyan friend who has TB, so we know how desperately she needs her medicine. We eagerly await the next shipment.

Our little school for orphaned and vulnerable children, developed by Christians in our Kikuyu community, is now taking in children from some of the camps for internally displaced people. Unfortunately, one year after the tribal clashes many families are still languishing in camps.

The rains did not come this year. Three million people face starvation as the drought holds on. The scorched Kenyan soil gives up very little sustenance to families who herd their cattle and scavenge for food and water.

Our neighbors have cut back on food for their children. As crops have failed, food prices have soared. Families are making do the best they can.

Nothing, we believe, can separate us from God's love. So how do Kenyans cope? How do they see God in their midst? They remember God's continuing faithfulness and lean on God's grace.

Life has no simple answers. The faith response to God's grace is trust, with a certainty that God cares and that God will provide. Christian maturity comes through our circumstances, and the circumstances here in Kenya are real and painful.

We can't say it is easy—it is miserable feeling helpless, helpless to change things, helpless to usher in a better world. Yet we share what we have and we do what we can to help.

Jesus Christ came into the same kind of world, and he said, "Fear not, for I have overcome the world." "My peace I give to you." The Holy Spirit, the Comforter is here, for God's love will never let us go.

—Rev. Dr. Lyle Dykstra and Terry Dykstra, PC(USA) mission volunteers

Daily Lectionary
☼ Ps. 119:73–80, 145 ☾ Ps. 121, 6
Gen. 37:1–11
1 Cor. 1:1–19; Mark 1:1–13

Prayer
Creator God, we pray for Kenyans and all people who suffer, that they may be sustained by God's love and grace. For "out of the believer's heart shall flow rivers of living water." Amen.

Democratic Republic of the Congo

During the 2007–2008 school year in Kinshasa, not once was school canceled for riots, demonstrations, or gunfire exchange in the city. For the first time in six years we made it through a school year without schools having to close due to political unrest in the capital. During that year we saw the economy pick up and an increase in goods available in the stores. Throughout the city new homes and businesses were built, and older ones

Workers making doors for new homes in Kinshasa are a sign of hope.

were remodeled. There were more vehicles on the road. It was as though people were making up for lost time. So much is possible in times of peace. With civil peace in Kinshasa, growth, optimism, and hope were able to spring up. How we wish that could be said for Eastern Congo! There are over two million Presbyterians in the Democratic Republic of the Congo, and on any given Sunday somewhere there is a church of believers praying for peace for their community and for their country. With the disarmament of militias, there are signs of resolution on the horizon. Let us join with our Congolese brothers and sisters in Christ in praying that peace will come, bringing healing and hope to so many who have known only violence, insecurity, and despair for too long.

—*Inge Sthreshley, PC(USA) mission co-worker*

Total area: 905,568 sq. mi. (slightly less than one-fourth the size of the United States). **Population:** 68,692,542. **Languages:** French (official), Lingala, Kingwana, Kikongo, Tshiluba. **GDP per capita:** $300. **Literacy:** 67.2% (male 80.9%, female 54.1%). **Religions:** Roman Catholic, Protestant, Kimbanguist, Muslim, other. **Life expectancy:** 54.36 years. **Human Development Index rank:** 177.

Prayer

Lord, we pray for peace in the Congo. Give wisdom and insight to those in positions of influence and power who are seeking solutions to conflict. Bind those who perpetrate evil. Bring comfort, healing, and hope to those who are victims of war. Encourage and strengthen your church in Congo to be an instrument of peace and healing. Amen.

Let us join in prayer for:

PC(USA) People in Mission
Presbyterian Community in Congo (CPC):
Gwenda Fletcher, education consultant, **Dr. John Fletcher**, surgical consultant, **Dr. Michael Haninger**, gynecologist/physician, **Nancy Haninger**, certified nurse midwife, **Inge Sthreshley**, team ministry, **Dr. Lawrence Sthreshley**, health consultant in Africa

PC(USA) General Assembly Staff
Richard H. C. Clay, FDN
Rev. Kerry Clements, OGA
Anita Clemons, FDN

Daily Lectionary
☼ Ps. 34, 146 ☾ Ps. 25, 91
Gen. 37:12–24
1 Cor. 1:20–31; Mark 1:14–28

Let us join in prayer for:

Partners/Ministries
Presbyterian Community of Kinshasa
(CPK): **Rev. Tshimungu Mayele,**
president communautaire • Presbyterian
Community of Congo (CPC): **Rev. Dr.
Mulumba M. Mukundi,** general secretary •
Sheppard and Lapsley Presbyterian
University of Congo (UPRECO):
Rev. Dr. Mulumba M. Mukundi, rector •
Protestant University of Congo (UPC):
Dr. Ngoy Boliya, rector • Presbytery
Partnerships: New Castle Presbytery,
Presbytery of Sheppards and Lapsley, and
Presbytery of Whitewater Valley with
CPC; Eastern Virginia with CPK; Mission
Presbytery with Luebo Hospital and CPC

PC(USA) General Assembly Staff
Hyunjoo Cline, GAMC
Charlene Coakley, GAMC

Democratic Republic of the Congo, *continued*

Congolese culture remains largely male dominated. In rural villages, often girls do not attend school and instead tend the household, work in the fields, and care for younger siblings. Girls as young as fourteen are sold into arranged marriages. The average village "bride price" is $50, or a medium-sized goat. Although women are the largest contributors to the family income, the males in the household generally control family funds. The practice of polygamy also oppresses women.

Survivors receive care and vocational training at a school in Tshikaji.

The scope of sexual and domestic violence against women and girls in the Democratic Republic of the Congo is well-known, documented and reported by media sources and international nongovernmental organizations. Girls who become pregnant through rape are often stigmatized and rejected by their families and communities. At times these young mothers are forced into prostitution in order to support themselves and their children.

In 2008 Dr. Augustin Mwala, director of the medical department in the Presbyterian Community of Congo, and women in the village of Tshikaji started a school to help support rape victims. Its one-year program seeks to provide a safe, loving, Christian environment where the girls can regain their self-worth and dignity while receiving training and education in machine sewing. In addition the girls take secondary school courses, all taught by three wonderful Congolese women. After nineteen single mothers completed the first class, each received a new sewing machine and supplies to start their own small business. Thirty new students are currently enrolled.

—*Nancy and Mike Haninger, PC(USA) mission co-workers*

Prayer
Dear God, on this day we ask for your special love and protection of girls and women in the Congo who every day suffer the extreme pain and humiliation of oppression and sexual violence. Amen.

Daily Lectionary
✿ Ps. 5, 147:1–11 ☾ Ps. 27, 51
Gen. 37:25–36
1 Cor. 2:1–13; Mark 1:29–45

Zimbabwe

Like much of southern Africa, Zimbabwe depends on life-giving rain that only falls from November to March. Her beleaguered citizens—those who haven't escaped from ten years of privation and political violence—can find sustenance as well in partnerships with those outside the country. Churches and homes proudly display photos, letters, and prayers. Many a resident queues at Western Union to pick up precious foreign currency sent from elsewhere by friends and relatives.

Football rules at Lovemore Home in Harare, where even the youngest boy can deliver a big kick.

The Presbytery of Denver has grown in relationship with the Presbytery of Zimbabwe (UPCSA). The presbyteries exchange messages, visitors, and resources. Currently, Denver is hosting the Neshangwes. While Lydia pursues theological study, Rev. Paul is developing a church. It is a win-win situation for both communions. By the time they go home, Lydia will be finished with school, so Zimbabwe will gain a strong female minister, and Rev. Paul will have developed a new African fellowship for the Presbytery of Denver.

Madison Avenue Presbyterian Church in New York City has been walking in partnership with the Synod of Harare (CCAP). For more than a decade, Lovemore Home in Harare has rescued lost boys from the streets. Though most have suffered traumatic abuse, today they live in Christian community, attend a good school, raise chickens, and grow vegetables. All of this is supported by Presbyterians in the United States. Partnership changes lives!

—*Sue and Ted Wright, former PC(USA) regional liaisons, South Central Africa*

Total area: 150,804 sq. mi. (slightly larger than Montana). **Population:** 11,392,629. **Languages:** English (official), tribal dialects. **GDP per capita:** $200. **Religions:** syncretic (part Christian, part indigenous beliefs), Christian, indigenous beliefs, Muslim, other. **Literacy:** 90.7% (male 94.2%, female 87.2%). **Life expectancy:** 45.77 years. **Human Development Index rank:** 151.

Prayer

Your word teaches, O Lord, that two are better than one, for they can gain a good reward from their toil. We bless you for all who do the good work of partnership, walking in the way, truth, and love of Jesus Christ. Amen.

Let us join in prayer for:

Partners/Ministries
Church of Central Africa Presbyterian (CCAP), Harare Synod: **Rev. Joseph Juma**, general secretary, **Rev. Lebias Boloma**, deputy general secretary • Uniting Presbyterian Church in Southern Africa (UPCSA), Presbytery of Zimbabwe: **Rev. Mark E. Philips**, presbytery clerk, **Rev. Wilbert Sayimani**, moderator, **Mrs. Norah Zidyana**, administrator • Zimbabwe Council of Churches: **Rev. Densen Mafinyani**, general secretary • Lovemore Home for Boys • Presbytery Partnership: Presbytery of Denver with UPCSA

PC(USA) General Assembly Staff
Patrick Cole, GAMC
Kenny Coleman, FDN
Charelle Collins, BOP

Daily Lectionary

☼ Ps. 27, 147:12–20 ☾ Ps. 126, 102
Gen. 39:1–23
1 Cor. 2:14—3:15; Mark 2:1–12

Let us join in prayer for:

Partners/Ministries
United Church of Zambia (UCZ):
Rev. Chrispin Mbalazi, general secretary •
Church of Central Africa Presbyterian
(CCAP), Synod of Zambia: **Rev. Daniel
Tembo**, moderator, **Rev. Victor Chilenje**,
vice-moderator, **Rev. Maleka Rabson
Kabendama**, general secretary,
Rev. Gerald Phiri, deputy general
secretary, **Mr. Isaac B. Ngulube**, general
treasurer • The Uniting Presbyterian
Church in Southern Africa (UPCSA),
Zambia Synod: **Rev. Thomson
Mkandawire**, moderator, **Rev. Sauros
Phaika**, clerk, **Elder Manuel Harawa**,
general treasurer • Christian Council of
Zambia: **Rev. Suzanne Matale**, general
secretary • Christian Hospital Association
of Zambia: **Ms. G. Haimbé**, director,
Mbreshi and Mwandi hospitals, Mindolo
Ecumenical Foundation: **Rev. Reuben
Daka**, director

PC(USA) General Assembly Staff
Emily Collins, OGA
Vennie Constant, GAMC

Daily Lectionary
☼ Ps. 22, 148 ☽ Ps. 105, 130
Gen. 40:1–23
1 Cor. 3:16–23; Mark 2:13–22

Zambia

The Rev. Thantiwe serves both as a pastor and a pastor's wife.

The Rev. Thantiwe, or TT Chipeta, rises before dawn to open the church and lead daily intercessory prayers. Though she is a pastor, she is married to a pastor and must also serve his congregation. Later she will conduct the ladies' guild meeting, visit the sick, and perhaps counsel troubled women—duties conferred through her role as wife. In her role as pastor, she travels to a parish some forty minutes away. She was twelve years old when she first felt the call. Although she trained alongside her husband, she was denied recognition for six years.

TT prays, "God, you know I am female, so I trust you for strength to carry on." Her daughters help with cooking, laundry, and carrying water. With little money for bus fare, TT often walks from one preaching point to the next. She understands why few sisters apply for ordination, but she smiles when she thinks about a childhood friend posted nearby.

She chooses her pulpit and teaching themes according to the church's weaknesses. Currently, prayer and giving top the list.

Please pray that her two children remaining in school can find employment, that a roof for the main congregation can be added, that the smallest preaching point can be revived, and that a third congregation can raise $1,000 to buy a plot of ground.

—*Sue and Ted Wright, former PC(USA) regional liaisons, South Central Africa*

Total area: 290,586 sq. mi. (slightly larger than Texas). **Population:** 11,862,740. **Languages:** English (official), 7 major vernaculars, about 70 other indigenous languages. **GDP per capita:** $1,500. **Literacy:** 80.6% (male 86.8%, female 74.8%). **Religions:** Christian, Muslim, and Hindu, indigenous beliefs. **Life expectancy:** 38.63 years. **Human Development Index rank:** 163.

Prayer

For humble, cheerful, and hardworking servants who answer your call, dear God, we bless your name. We lift up especially our sisters in ministry, who do Mary and Martha work combined. For Jesus' sake. Amen.

Malawi

On morning rounds at Mulanje Mission Hospital in Malawi, one of my patients seemed especially worried, and she pulled on my sleeve for attention. She whispered, "I don't have any clothes for my babies."

My heart went out to her as I looked at her precious newborn twins, wrapped only in thin cloth. I felt God's grace and love as I was able to tell her that our mission hospital would be happy to give her some clothes and blankets for the babies. Faithful Presbyterians regularly send donations to our hospital for this very purpose.

A mother's heart overflows with joy when her babies are healthy and have warm clothes.

Jeremiah 1:5 (NIV) tells us, "Before I formed you in the womb I knew you, before you were born I set you apart." God's love and God's purposes for us begin before we are even born. We can remember that God is always with us, even from the moment of our birth, even before birth. What a thought for an obstetrician!

—*Sue Makin, PC(USA) mission co-worker*

Total area: 45,745 sq. mi. (slightly smaller than Pennsylvania). **Population:** 14,268,711. **Languages:** Chichewa (official), Chinyanja, Chiyao, other regional languages. **GDP per capita:** $800. **Literacy:** 62.7% (male 76.1%, female 49.8%). **Religions:** Christian, Muslim, other. **Life expectancy:** 43.82 years. **Human Development Index rank:** 162.

Prayer

Lord, you taught us to consider the lilies, how they grow, without toiling and spinning. You told us not to be anxious. Lord, your love surrounds us and enfolds us. Help us to share this love around the world. Amen.

Let us join in prayer for:

PC(USA) People in Mission
Church of Central Africa Presbyterian (CCAP): **Rev. Deborah Chase**, dean of academic affairs and lecturer, Livingstonia Synod, **Rev. Mary Catherine (Kay) Day**, training chaplain/Chigodi administrator, Blantyre Synod, **Darlene Heller**, matron of crisis nursery, Ministry of Hope, Livingstonia Synod, **Rev. Paul Heller**, director of crisis nursery, Ministry of Hope, Livingstonia Synod, **Dr. Mary (Sue) Makin**, obstetrician/gynecologist, Blantyre Synod, **James McGill**, water sanitation and development specialist, Livingstonia Synod, **Jodi McGill**, clinical instructor of nursing, Livingstonia Synod, **Dr. Barbara Nagy**, physician, Nkoma Synod, **Dr. Martha Sommers**, medical officer, Livingstonia Synod

PC(USA) General Assembly Staff
Chris Conver, PPC
Judith Coons, GAMC
Debra Cooper, BOP

The Lord's Day

Minute for Mission: Camp and Conference Ministries

On a day like today, it could be hard to imagine the impending change of seasons. As the starkness of winter turns to the green of spring, the beauty of God's creation blossoms at the 140 Presbyterian camps and conference centers across the United States. The natural surroundings in these special places come alive for a new year of ministry. It is on these pieces of sacred ground that church groups gather for retreats, children and youth come together for summer camp, and youth and adults from across the country meet for conference experiences.

There is no need to tell you about the power of these experiences. Statistics show that Presbyterians, like all Christians, find "living water" at camp and conference experiences. When they remove themselves from a world of distractions, they can see more clearly the way God is working in their lives and in the midst of their communities. These participants return to the world with a renewed heart for ministry and a deeper understanding of themselves. Camp and conference ministry touches the lives of all ages and is an incredible example

Calvin Crest Conferences

Summer campers participate in the sunrise worship on top of Fresno Dome in the Sierra National Forest.

of what we can do to grow Christ's church through evangelism and discipleship.

As February comes to a close, it is a good time for us to pray for the important ministry that takes place at our Presbyterian camps and conference centers each year. You can go to www.pccca.net and learn more about the sacred spaces in your state or region.

—*Joel Winchip, executive director, Presbyterian Church Camp and Conference Association, York, South Carolina*

Prayer

Creator God, we thank you for the changing seasons and for the beauty of your creation. Please be with the staff and volunteers at our Presbyterian camps and conference centers as they prepare the programs and maintain the facilities. We thank you for the lives that will be transformed at these special places this year. It is in the name of your son, Jesus Christ, that we pray. Amen.

Malawi, *continued*

Embangweni Hospital is one of the Synod of Livingstonia's three hospitals. Embangweni consists of the main 130-bed hospital, four health centers, twenty mobile clinics, and other village health services. The Synod of Livingstonia is in a long-standing partnership with the Presbyterian Church (U.S.A.). As a mission co-worker, I am a gift of this partnership and serve as the only long-term doctor at Embangweni Hospital, which serves roughly 100,000 people.

Head nurse Catherine Mzembe settles a new mother with the help of her guardian as another patient looks on.

I work with about two hundred dedicated Malawian Christians, representing some ten denominations, who compassionately and competently serve the suffering who come to us.

Maternal death is one of Malawi's biggest challenges: one woman dies per one hundred births, and one woman dies per fifty Caesarean sections. Annually 3,000 babies are born at Embangweni, where the maternal death rate is about one-sixth that of the rest of the country. Our success comes from the efforts of many believers working together, flowing together, for life: from those who donate blood at a moment's notice, to those who donate funds so that we have medicines and can pay staff; from churches that provide funds to extend the maternity ward, to the local volunteers who mold the bricks; from the nurse midwives who work most of their days off so the maternity ward can be staffed, to home health workers who have been teaching expectant mothers at the mobile clinics in the villages for some thirty years—so many believers' efforts flow together with the help of the Holy Spirit.

—*Martha Sommers, PC(USA) mission co-worker*

Prayer

Jesus, please open our hearts so that we respond to those who are suffering. Teach us to join our efforts with other believers to work for life and to glorify your name. Amen.

Let us join in prayer for:

Partners/Ministries
Church of Central Africa Presbyterian (CCAP), General Assembly • CCAP, Blantyre Synod: **Rev. Macdonald Kadawati**, general secretary, **Rev. Andrew Maere**, deputy general secretary, **Rev. Rodney Bona**, moderator • CCAP, Livingstonia Synod: **Rev. M. Mezuwa Banda**, moderator, **Rev. Levi N. Nyondo**, general secretary, **Rev. Maurice C. E. Munthali**, deputy general secretary • CCAP, Nkhoma Synod: **Rev. Davidson Chifungo**, general secretary, **Rev. Chatha Msangaambe**, moderator • Ekwendeni, Embangweni, David Gordon, Mulanje, and Nkhoma hospitals • Malawi Council of Churches: **Rev. Dr. Augustine C. Musopole**, general secretary • Zomba Theological College: **Rev. Staples Mazizwa**, principal, **Rev. Joseph A. Thipa**, vice principal, **Rev. Takuze S. Chitsulo**, dean • Presbytery Partnerships: Presbytery of Eastern Oklahoma and Presbytery of Northern New York with CCAP, Livingstonia Synod; Pittsburgh Presbytery with CCAP, Blantyre Synod

PC(USA) General Assembly Staff
Catherine Cottingham, GAMC
Audrey Cotten, OGA

Daily Lectionary

☼ Ps. 119:73–80, 145 ☾ Ps. 121, 6
Gen. 41:46–57
1 Cor. 4:8–20 (21); Mark 3:7–19a

Let us join in prayer for:

Partners/Ministries
Presbyterian Church of Mozambique:
Rev. Jonas Ngomane, moderator,
Rev. Ernesto Langa, administrator,
Rev. Oriente Sibane, president of synod
council • Christian Council of Mozambique:
Rev. Lucas Amosse, general secretary •
Ricatla Seminary [Mozambique] •
Presbyterian Church of Mauritius:
Rev. France Cangy, moderator,
Mrs. Margaret Fayolle, president

PC(USA) General Assembly Staff
Jennifer Cox, PPC
Carla Coyle, FDN
Jean Coyle, GAMC

Daily Lectionary
☼ Ps. 34, 146 ☾ Ps. 25, 91
Gen. 42:1–17
1 Cor. 5:1–8; Mark 3:19b–35

Mozambique

Fernando served in the army for seven years. He writes, "I came to Christ while I was a soldier. I prayed among Presbyterians." After demobilization he took a two-year certificate course in Maputo and went to work for a large congregation.

But his heart still longed for the rural north—for the Zambezi Valley where he had been raised. So he joined a project of holistic evangelism supported by The Outreach Foundation. There he worked with two pastors who had connections at Justo Mwale, a Reformed theological college in Zambia. Fernando's experience, and his vision for growing the church, made him a natural candidate when space opened at Justo Mwale for another Presbyterian from Mozambique.

—Sue and Ted Wright, former PC(USA)
regional liaisons, South Central Africa

Total area: 309,496 sq. mi. (slightly less than twice the size of California). **Population:** 21,669,278. **Languages:** Emakhuwa, Portuguese (official), other indigenous languages. **GDP per capita:** $900. **Literacy:** 47.8% (male 63.5%, female 32.7%). **Religions:** Catholic, Zionist Christian, other. **Life expectancy:** 41.18 years. **Human Development Index rank:** 175.

Mauritius

Forty years ago the economy of Mauritius was largely agricultural. Today new tourism, financial services, and call center industries have eclipsed older ways of life. Economic transformation has also meant changes to work patterns. Many people employed in round-the-clock industries find it difficult to take part in Sunday morning worship services. The small but vibrant Presbyterian Church of Mauritius has responded by exploring new forms of worship and fellowship. St. Andre's parish in Beau Bassin, for example, has established a series of house churches on weekday evenings to enable shift workers to share in the life and witness of the congregation.

—Doug Tilton, PC(USA) regional liaison, Southern Africa

Total area: 788 sq. mi. (almost 11 times the size of Washington, DC). **Population:** 1,284,264. **Languages:** Creole, Bhojpuri, English and French (official), other. **GDP per capita:** $12,100. **Literacy:** 84.4% (male 88.4%, female 80.5%). **Religions:** Hindu, Roman Catholic, Muslim, other Christian, other. **Life expectancy:** 74 years. **Human Development Index rank:** 74

Prayer
Thank you, O God, that you have great plans for all of us and that you walk with us through times of change and uncertainty. Give us new eyes so that we may see how you work afresh in each new situation. Help us to follow your lead in all things. Amen.

Madagascar

Finding clean water in Tsaramiakatra, a village fifty miles from Madagascar's capital, Antananarivo, has long been a difficult and unreliable process. With the help of PC(USA) mission co-worker Elizabeth Turk and Faith Presbyterian Church in Tallahassee, Florida, the Development Department (SAF) of the Church of Jesus Christ in Madagascar brought the water of life to Tsaramiakatra and two neighboring villages. Several years ago, community leaders asked SAF

A young Tsaramiakatra resident fetches water from one of the five taps installed by SAF and the PC(USA).

Doug Tilton

for assistance in developing a potable water source. SAF helped residents to survey the site and to plan a reservoir and gravity-fed system that could supply safe drinking water to all three villages. In 2006 Faith Presbyterian Church raised the funds to cover the installation. A mission team travelled to Madagascar to assist with the work, which was completed in 2007.

The initiative has not only brought safe drinking water to the villages, but it has enabled residents to tap an ever-flowing stream of blessings. The communities have also built latrines and showers that mean improved hygiene for all. SAF has provided residents with mosquito nets to fight malaria and shared information on nutrition, HIV and AIDS, family planning, and other public health topics. According to many of Tsaramiakatra's women, though, the greatest gift has been the time saved. "Now we can spend more time with our children and families," they said. "And we have more time for God."

—Doug Tilton, PC(USA) regional liaison for Southern Africa

Total area: 226,657 sq. mi. (slightly less than twice the size of Arizona). **Population:** 20,653,556. **Languages:** English, French, and Malagasy (all official). **GDP per capita:** $1,000. **Literacy:** 68.9% (male 75.5%, female 62.5%). **Religions:** indigenous beliefs, Christian, Muslim. **Life expectancy:** 62.89 years. **Human Development Index rank:** 143.

Prayer

Loving God, we give you thanks for the water that sustains all life. Help us to care for each other, so that your people shall never thirst but may be eternally refreshed by the crystal streams of justice and righteousness that flow from your throne. Amen.

Wednesday, March 3

Let us join in prayer for:

PC(USA) People in Mission
Church of Jesus Christ in Madagascar (FJKM): **Elizabeth Turk**, public health specialist, **Robert (Dan) Turk**, environment/development

Partners/Ministries
FJKM: **Rev. Lala Rasendrahasina**, president, **Mr. Marc Ravalomanana** and **Dr. Laurent Ramambason**, vice-presidents, **Rev. Marinasy**, general secretary • Akany Avoko Home for Girls • Federation of Protestant Churches in Madagascar: **Rev. Edmond Razafimanantsoa**, general secretary • Synod Partnership: Synod of the Northeast with the FJKM

PC(USA) General Assembly Staff
Barry Creech, GAMC
Lindsay Crosby, BOP

Daily Lectionary

☼ Ps. 5, 147:1–11; ☾ Ps. 27, 51
Gen. 42:18–28
1 Cor. 5:9—6:11; Mark 4:1–20

Lesotho

It was the first of the year. School fees for the older children were due. Sixty of the children needed new shoes, and twenty-five needed new uniforms. The babies were running out of formula and the cupboards were almost bare. One hundred and fourteen children in this little orphan care center in Maseru, Lesotho, would go hungry if God didn't do something fast.

Children at an orphan care center in Maseru were blessed with an unexpected gift that arrived just in time.

And then, on the sixteenth of January, a gift was wired into the local account—a huge gift—more than enough to refill the cupboards, outfit the children, and get them into school on time.

The source? A one-day visitor who had enjoyed a romp on the floor of the baby room with a couple of doe-eyed little ones. She was an artist. And she had taken their picture, painted it, printed it, sold it. And now, one year later, she sent the proceeds to provide for their needs and those of the others in the orphan care center—just when they needed it most. God's perfect provision and perfect timing. To him be all the glory. "Before they call I will answer, while they are yet speaking I will hear" (Isa. 65:24).

—*Nancy Dimmock, PC(USA) mission co-worker*

Total area: 11,720 sq. mi. (slightly smaller than Maryland). **Population:** 2,130,819. **Languages:** Sesotho, English (official), Zulu, Xhosa. **GDP per capita:** $1,600. **Literacy:** 84.8% (male 74.5%, female 94.5%). **Religions:** Christian, indigenous beliefs. **Life expectancy:** 40.38 years. **Human Development Index rank:** 155.

Prayer
Loving God, thank you that you know our needs before we can even ask and that you provide answers at the perfect time. We ask that you would watch over all children in need and remind us of our responsibilities to those who live without the warmth or security of your love. Amen.

World Day of Prayer

Minute for Mission

Fifteen years ago I was part of a group that had the privilege of visiting Cameroon, where Presbyterians have been involved in mission for more than a century and where strong Presbyterian churches continue that witness today. As part of this trip we went to Metet, site of a well-known Presbyterian mission hospital.

Lydia Belle Efimba, ecumenical delegate from the Presbyterian Church of Cameroon, participates in the 217th General Assembly (2006).

While the medical people were busy discussing the kinds of surgeries and medical procedures provided by the hospital, one of the women (who could tell that I really didn't have much to contribute to that conversation) suggested that I might come with her to see something more interesting. We walked for about a mile through a gorgeous jungle and came upon a small Presbyterian church where the women were holding a prayer service. They told me when I entered the church that "prayer is what really changes things around here" and invited me to join them. Then they prayed for me and my family. I felt a special closeness to God that afternoon.

Today is the World Day of Prayer, and the focus this year is on Cameroon. The World Day of Prayer movement launched by women in the nineteenth century involves Christians in over 170 countries who pray together for people in a particular part of the world—this year for women in Cameroon. I hope that you will join in this movement today. As you do, I hope that you will remember our sisters in Cameroon and that you will find the theme of the World Day of Prayer movement—"Informed prayer leads to prayerful action"—to be true for you.

—*Rev. Clifton Kirkpatrick, president, World Alliance of Reformed Churches*

Prayer

Gracious God, we join millions of other Christians around the world today in praising you and praying for a world made new. We pray especially for women in Cameroon, giving thanks for their faithful witness to the gospel in a difficult situation. May your Holy Spirit unite us all in prayer for the life in fullness for all people that you promise in Jesus Christ, in whose name we pray. Amen.

Let us join in prayer for:

PC(USA) People in Mission
Rev. Janet Guyer, Southern Africa AIDS consultant, Evangelical Presbyterian Church of Southern Africa • **Rev. Bridgette Hector**, companionship facilitator, Joining Hands • **Dr. Douglas Tilton**, regional liaison, Southern Africa, World Mission

PC(USA) General Assembly Staff
Elder April Davenport, GAMC
Kathleen Davenport, BOP

South Africa

God's grace flows through our lives like a river, connecting people across distances and buoying us along on a common journey of faith and witness. When Phindile Madonsela formally opened the Sinenhlanhla Support Group outreach center amid joyful singing and ululation, it was a powerful sign of God's healing grace and call to partnership.

Phindi Madonsela (center, with arm raised), members of Sinenhlanhla, and partners celebrate the opening of the outreach center.

Phindi started the group after learning that she was living with HIV. She found that one of the most difficult aspects of being HIV positive was the isolation she experienced because she was expected to keep silent about her status. Sinenhlanhla was a way to break the silence, for individuals to help one another to live healthy and positive lives, and to give those living with HIV a place of safety and healing.

St. Columba's Uniting Presbyterian Church in Johannesburg shared Phindi's vision. Together with Worthington Presbyterian Church in Columbus, Ohio—which has long supported St. Columba's HIV and AIDS ministries— St. Columba's helped Sinenhlanhla renovate an unused building on the grounds of a high school in Soweto to provide office, meeting, and workshop space. The center enabled them to move out of Phindi's mother's home; allows the group to provide advice and counseling services to the wider community; and serves as a base for their gardening, beadwork, and shoemaking initiatives.

—*Doug Tilton, PC(USA) regional liaison, Southern Africa*

Total area: 471,011 sq. mi. (slightly less than twice the size of Texas). **Population:** 49,052,489. **Languages:** IsiXhosa, IsiZulu, Afrikaans, English, Sepedi, other. **GDP per capita:** $10,000. **Literacy:** 86.4. **Religions:** Zion Christian, other Christian, Muslim. **Life expectancy:** 48.98 years. **Human Development Index rank:** 125.

Prayer

God, our Sustainer, give us the courage to step into the healing streams of your grace and to share with all of your people the refreshment and renewal that we find there. Open our ears that we may hear the ways we are being called to work together to ensure that all may enjoy the life abundant promised in Christ. Amen.

The Lord's Day

Minute for Mission: Celebrate the Gifts of Women

Sunday, March 7

Sunday Lectionary and Hymns

Isa. 55:1–9
O for a Closer Walk with God
PH 396, 397, HB 319

Ps. 63:1–8
O Lord, You Are My God
PH 199
O Lord, My God, Most Earnestly
HB 327

1 Cor. 10:1–13
O God, Our Faithful God
PH 277

Luke 13:1–9
Kind Maker of the World
PH 79

In a book titled *The Future for Wo/Men*, one of the co-authors, Marchiene Reinstra, writes of a time she was walking on a forest path and came across a sign that read: "The human race is like a bird trying to fly with one wing. Until women fly alongside men using all their gifts, this bird cannot fly."

The image of this bird has drifted into my thoughts, dreams, and prayers ever since I read it. It seems to me that the church has a tremendous opportunity and calling to celebrate and promote the gifts of women, to soar through the world as an example of what it is to be the body of Christ, women and men together pouring forth the gifts of the Spirit.

Unfortunately, within the church (as within the human race in general) there has been some resistance to allowing both wings to stretch wide and support the body in mutuality and equality. As those who are set free by the Spirit of life in Christ Jesus, people of the church are called to display the fullness of that life to all. This can only be done with both wings lifted in flight, with the gifts of women celebrated and utilized as fully as the gifts of men.

> *Until women fly alongside men using all their gifts, this bird cannot fly.*

Throughout history we can see the witness of God's activity in the lives and gifts of women. Today we name and celebrate those gifts, both those that have been acknowledged and promoted and those who have been silenced by resistance. We live in the hope that filled by the Spirit, we will one day soar, bolstered on each side by the gifts God gives to all of God's children.

—*Courtney J. Hoekstra, staff support, Advocacy Committee for Women's Concerns, General Assembly Mission Council*

Prayer

Even the sparrow finds a home, and the swallow a nest for herself at your altars, holy God. As the sparrow flies to you with both wings outstretched, give your church the wisdom to do your work using both wings. Forgive us for those times we intentionally or unintentionally clip the wing of women's gifts. In the name of Christ, the One in whose image both women and men have been created. Amen.

Daily Lectionary

☼ Ps. 84, 150 ☾ Ps. 42, 32
Gen. 44:1–17
Rom. 8:1–10; John 5:25–29

Let us join in prayer for:

Partners/Ministries
South African Council of Churches:
Mr. Eddie Makue, general secretary,
Prof. Tinyiko Maluleke, president •
Evangelical Presbyterian Church in South
Africa (EPCSA): **Rev. H. Dixon Masangu**,
moderator, **Rev. Titus R. Mobbie**, general
secretary • Presbyterian Church of Africa:
Rev. Eric Matomela, moderator, **Rev. W.
Mzukisi Faleni**, stated clerk • Uniting
Presbyterian Church in South Africa
(UPCSA): **Rev. Christopher Mkandawire**,
moderator, **Rev. Dr. Jerry Pillay**, general
secretary • Uniting Reformed Church in
South Africa (URCSA): **Prof. S. T. Kgatla**,
moderator, **Dr. Dawid Kuyler**, general
secretary • Presbytery Partnerships:
Presbytery of Boise, Presbytery of Donegal,
Presbytery of Florida, Presbytery of New
York City, North Alabama Presbytery, and
Presbytery of Northern New England with
the UPCSA; Presbytery of Western New
York with the URCSA; Presbytery of the
Western Reserve with Sisonke Masilwe
Indlala through Joining Hands

PC(USA) General Assembly Staff
Deb Davies, OGA
Gloria Davis, GAMC
Gloria Davis, BOP

South Africa, *continued*

In southern Africa we are living where AIDS has struck the hardest. It is a part of everyone's life. We have all lost loved ones to the HIV virus. So, one might ask, where are those rivers of living water in the midst of this pandemic?

We are holding a series of workshops on HIV and AIDS in a presbytery of the Evangelical Presbyterian Church in South Africa. On the first day we asked participants why they chose to attend and to make a commitment of six weekends. Sylvia said she wanted to make a difference in her community and in her church. As time went on, she told me her story.

Sylvia, an HIV/AIDS home-based care provider, participates in a training workshop.

When Sylvia's daughter was thirteen, she was lured into a relationship with an older man who wanted sex with a young girl. In hindsight Sylvia is aware that her daughter had enough knowledge about HIV and AIDS to know that what she was doing put her at risk, but not the skills to refuse him. That year she became infected with HIV. Eight years later her daughter got sick. Sylvia nursed her intensively until her death.

Today the pain of her loss is still there, but so is something else. Born of her faith and her commitment to serve God's people, Sylvia is providing home-based care for ten people with AIDS. She's using the skills she learned caring for her daughter, the love and compassion that bring hope when it seems hopeless, and a touch of peace in the midst of suffering and grief . . . living waters from the heart of God.

—*Janet Guyer, PC(USA) regional AIDS consultant, Southern Africa*

Daily Lectionary
☼ Ps. 119:73–80, 145 ☾ Ps. 121, 6
Gen. 44:18–34
1 Cor. 7:25–31; Mark 5:21–43

Prayer
Loving God, walk with us in our times of pain and show us how we can be your hands and heart reaching out to those around us—to be the channel for your rivers of living water in our world. Amen.

The Synod of Alaska-Northwest

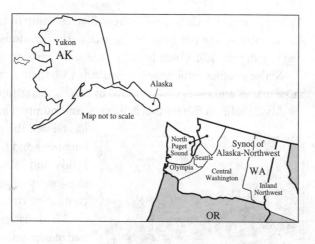

Map not to scale

What happens when a heart is cold and icy, when the gift of faith lies fallow and unexplored? Two young men came to Rainbow Glacier Camp in Haines, Alaska, for a week of Christian camping. By the end of the week the counselors were absolutely stumped at the boys' behavior. Their hearts appeared truly hardened. At the final worship service in the outdoor chapel that overlooks the Chilkat River and looks up to the Rainbow Glacier, two miracles took place. In the middle of worship a huge chunk of glacier calved, filling the air with a thunderous crash. Then a hummingbird flew into camp and hovered in front of only two faces. Which two? The two boys who had been impervious to the gospel all week were overcome by God, who knew and loved them. Their hearts melted. The hearts of two believers began to beat.

The Synod of Alaska-Northwest gratefully embraces the camping and conference ministries that support the 269 congregations and 57,512 members in their spiritual practices of retreat, evangelism, and prayer. The synod is home to Bingle Memorial Camp, Clearwater Lodge and Camp Spalding, the Campbell Farm, Ghormley Meadow Christian Camp, Sound View Camp and Retreat Center, and Tall Timber Ranch, in addition to Rainbow Glacier Camp.

Prayer

Holy God, our hearts become heavy with the burdens of life. Then you break into our despair with a simple gift from nature or a word from Scripture, and we know that you are working in, around, and through us. Thank you. In Jesus' name. Amen.

Let us join in prayer for:

Synod Staff
Rev. Joyce Martin Emery, transitional synod executive
Elder Alma-jean Marion, coordinator of administrative ministry
Elder Sarah Peniston, director of communications
Dean Mielke, director, mission development certificate program
Linda Paulson, loan processor/accounting clerk
Robert MacDonald, comptroller

PC(USA) General Assembly Staff
Trina Deluca, BOP
Jonathan Dennis, GAMC
Sheldon Dennis, BOP

Daily Lectionary
☉ Ps. 34, 146 ☾ Ps. 25, 91
Gen. 45:1–15
1 Cor. 7:32–40; Mark 6:1–13

Wednesday, March 10

Let us join in prayer for:

Presbytery Staff
David Dobler, pastor to the presbytery
Cyndi Gleason, office manager
Venus Zink, treasurer

PC(USA) General Assembly Staff
Terry Dennis, BOP
Elder Lionel Derenoncourt, GAMC

The Presbytery of Alaska

The fifteen churches and Rainbow Glacier Camp of the Presbytery of Alaska are strung like pearls along the archipelago of southeast Alaska. They are tied together by 1,053 members, by the sea, by mission, and by Christ.

Native peoples settled these coastlands with their cedar canoes, Presbyterian missionaries and evangelists traveled by canoe, steamship, and mission boat, and the Alaska salmon fishery touched every community. This rich cultural history has blessed the presbytery with Native languages and traditions of the Tlingit, Haida, and Tsimshian peoples, missionary adventure stories, and the continuing rhythms of season and tides.

The mission boat Anna Jackman cruises near Sitka and Mt. Edgecomb.

Missionaries from the lower 48 and native evangelists spread the gospel in towns, fishing camps, and logging communities. Mission boats were built and deployed, with names evoking the mission heritage, such as the *Toronado*, won in a poker game by Rev. Bromely of Haines, and the *Marietta*, skippered by Edward Marsden of Metlakatla, the first Alaska Native ordained with college and seminary training. Various communities took pride in provisioning a mission boat for a season.

Today Alaskan logging is virtually nonexistent. The changing politics and economics of fishing have undercut the livelihood of many villages, but the people and the church remain. The example and experience of earlier generations inspire efforts to be effective missionaries today. Financial sustainability is one challenge, with the passing of the national mission system. Finding new ways to train and support pastors and caring for the presbytery's historic churches nestled in the rainforest are others. Constant through these changes are the mission of Christ and the promise of God's providence.

Prayer

Lord Jesus Christ, we thank you for the ministry to youth and young adults at Rainbow Glacier Camp. We ask that the congregations of the Presbytery of Alaska continue constant in your service and abide in your peace. Amen.

Daily Lectionary

☼ Ps. 5, 147:1–11 ☾ Ps. 27, 51
Gen. 45:16–28
1 Cor. 8:1–13; Mark 6:13–29

The Presbytery of Central Washington

Let us join in prayer for:

Presbytery Staff
Rev. G. David Lambertson, executive presbyter
Deborah Dawson, administrative assistant
Elder Kenneth A. Gasper, stated clerk
Stan Fishburn, director, Tall Timber Ranch
Mark Washam, director, Ghormley Meadow Christian Camp

PC(USA) General Assembly Staff
Shari DeVonish, GAMC
Stanley DeVoogd, GAMC
Diane Dewees, GAMC

In January 2006 Meadow Springs Presbyterian Church in Richland embarked on a "Journey of Discovery." A four-year process, it was created through a cooperative project of the presbyteries of Yellowstone, Glacier, Inland Northwest, and Central Washington and the Center for Parish Development to support churches engaging in missional transformation. The purpose of the process is to help churches design, plan, and manage a major transition into faithful and effective missional churches in a secularized culture. The emphasis throughout this process is on Bible study and believing that the church is the called people of God who are sent to be a sign, foretaste, and instrument of God's kingdom of heaven and earth.

For the Meadow Springs Church the journey is led by pastor Bob Johnson, parish associate Richard Nordgren, and elders Diana Redetzke, David and Leota Hallyburton, and Travis McClelland, who function as the coordinating team. During each phase they have developed Bible studies, regularly led the congregation in prayer during worship, conducted interviews for a diagnostic analysis, designed congregational retreats, and helped in writing a vision portrait for the congregation. They are now implementing the churches' vision and mission.

The Journey of Discovery has blessed the congregation with increased worship attendance, new members and ministries, participation in Bible study groups, prayer, and fellowship activities. The Sunday evening Bible study brings many young families together to deepen their spiritual journey. Meadow Springs Presbyterian Church is being transformed into a vibrant, active congregation that experiences joy in being the people of God. As its vision portrait states, "Meadow Springs Presbyterian Church is an A.C.T.S. church: where our prayers of Adoration, Confession, Thanksgiving, and Supplication guide our lives."

Children attending vacation Bible school are likely to sing "I've got a river of life, flowing out of me." Adults know the river is the Spirit of God springing up in their transforming church—the abundant life that Jesus promises to bring.

Meadow Springs is one of 42 churches in the Presbytery of Central Washington, which comprises a presbytery-wide membership of 7,070.

Prayer

Creator of Life, we give you thanks for your Spirit that quickens us to new life and fellowship in your church. May all of our journeys draw us closer to your Son and our Savior. Amen.

Daily Lectionary
☼ Ps. 27, 147:12–20 ☾ Ps. 126, 102
Gen. 46:1–7, 28–34
1 Cor. 9:1–15; Mark 6:30–46

Let us join in prayer for:

Presbytery Staff
Rev. Frank Beattie, interim
executive presbyter
Joyce Bippes, administrative assistant
Michael Copas, financial administrator
Elder Richard Welch,
presbytery moderator
Elder David Hamilton, stated clerk

PC(USA) General Assembly Staff
Bharat Dhillon, BOP
Lydia Diehl, GAMC

Daily Lectionary

☼ Ps. 22, 148 ☾ Ps. 105, 130
Gen. 47:1–26
1 Cor. 9:16–27; Mark 6:47–56

The Presbytery of the Inland Northwest

Idaho, Washington

First Presbyterian Church of Clarkston, Washington, believes caring for children is inherent to the call of Jesus Christ. In September 2009 First Presbyterian began its seventh year of T.L.C. (The Learning Club). Each fall T.L.C. is there for children who need a boost of confidence and help in getting into the learning mode.

In 2003 the interim pastor and the session sought an outreach into the community. One of the members had seen rewarding results from a program at Grantham Elementary School. It provided time each day for fourth grade children to read a book with engaged adults who listened and talked with them about the book. These children were increasingly benefiting from school.

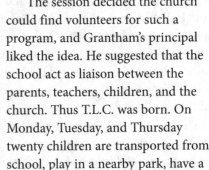

Annice Edmundson reads with Merrilyn Gunst, a T.L.C. student.

The session decided the church could find volunteers for such a program, and Grantham's principal liked the idea. He suggested that the school act as liaison between the parents, teachers, children, and the church. Thus T.L.C. was born. On Monday, Tuesday, and Thursday twenty children are transported from school, play in a nearby park, have a snack, and then get together with volunteers who come from First Presbyterian and neighboring churches. These adults help them with homework, read with them, hear about their lives, and try to reflect Christ's love.

The church, school staff, volunteers, children, and their families are excited each fall about new opportunities to help children learn how to use the gifts God has given them. Cheryl Jurgens has been coordinator of T.L.C. since 2006.

The Presbytery of the Inland Northwest works with 8,316 members in its 49 congregations.

Prayer

Father, we give thanks for bringing these children to T.L.C. Give volunteers the wisdom to guide them, patience to teach them, and vigilance to be role models of your love through example. Give them ears to listen, hearts to love, and energy to excite these children in their tasks. We ask this in your name, through Christ our Lord. Amen.

The Presbytery of North Puget Sound

Washington

In Africa thirst, both physical and spiritual, is very real. In pursuit of the desire to know God's will and direction, the Presbytery of North Puget Sound's Mountain View Church in Marysville sent a team to Senegal, West Africa. The team's goal was to find a group of people who were open to and thirsty for the Holy Spirit. After meeting with several villages, the team was introduced to the village

Members of Mountain View Church make new friends in Diagle, Senegal.

of Diagle. The team found the people of Diagle both open and eager to hear from their new friends, who quickly realized that God had been at work in Diagle long before this meeting.

Led by the Holy Spirit, Mountain View decided to follow what was clearly a calling from God to commit to a long-term relationship with the village of Diagle. This decision was made with an understanding that the privilege of sharing Christ with someone only comes after earning the right to be heard. The people of Diagle are members of the Wolof tribe, and in the Wolof culture the message is always tied to the messenger. To share a message of significance requires a strong relationship. Mountain View's long-term goal for this mission is to see a thriving church in Diagle made up of Wolof believers who can spread the living water of hope and quench the thirst of their people. Mountain View will be working in cooperation with several full-time missionaries, building on the work they have done. With God's guidance, living water will flow in Diagle.

There are 35 churches and 1 worshiping fellowship serving 7,521 members in the Presbytery of North Puget Sound. Tall Timber Ranch and Presbyterian-related Renewal Ministries Northwest, Tierra Nueva, and Eagle Wings disAbility Ministries are within the presbytery's bounds.

Prayer

Gracious God, through your Holy Spirit you lead us into new friendships with thirsty people. As we seek to share the message of your significance with others, equip us with humility and a willingness to invest in long-term, life-giving relationships. In Jesus' name. Amen.

Let us join in prayer for:

L. Clarence Antioquia, member, GAMC

Presbytery Staff
Dr. Corey Schlosser-Hall, executive presbyter
Rev. Dean Strong, stated clerk
Sarah Beard, communications coordinator
Joan Hill, financial coordinator

PC(USA) General Assembly Staff
Dawn Diggs, FDN
Carla Dobson, FDN

Daily Lectionary

✡ Ps. 43, 149 ☾ Ps. 31, 143
Gen. 47:27—48:7
1 Cor. 10:1–13; Mark 7:1–23

Sunday Lectionary and Hymns

Josh. 5:9–12
Now Thank We All Our God
PH 555, HB 9

Ps. 32
How Blest Are Those
PH 184, HB 281

2 Cor. 5:16–21
God, You Spin the Whirling Planets
PH 285

Luke 15:1–3, 11b–32
O Christ, the Healer
PH 380

Daily Lectionary

☼ Ps. 84, 150 ☾ Ps. 42, 32
Gen. 48:8–22
Rom. 8:11–25; John 6:27–40

The Lord's Day

Minute for Mission: Columbia Theological Seminary

If anyone is in Christ, there is a new creation: everything old has passed away; see, everything has become new! (2 Cor. 5:17).

What is the center of your life? What rules how you live? When Jesus walked the earth, he entered a world where people's hearts were ruled by many things other than God. He found religious leaders whose lives were centered on tradition and theology and who could see nothing beyond that,

The way of Christ is life-igniting.

and he found "sinners" who could only see life through the lens of their outcast status. Hierarchy had been established, and there was nearly no opportunity to transcend structural constraints. It seemed that self-understanding was determined by ideas and practices beyond their voluntary control.

Jesus came with a mission to change what was at the center of people's lives. Instead of ideas and practices that were life-diminishing and life-smothering, Jesus revealed a way that was life-igniting. It is available for us today. This is certainly good news!

In today's Gospel lesson, we see people whose lives were centered on tradition grumbling about Jesus' association with "tax collectors and sinners," the outcasts. Jesus tells them the parable of the prodigal son and his brother, and in the story challenges them to see the way that is life-igniting.

What is the center of your life? One thing is certain: if you make God your center, your life will not be diminished. You will find, as Paul says in 2 Corinthians, that you are a new creation. You will find the abundant life.

—*John Ruehl, M.Div. 2010, Columbia Theological Seminary*

Prayer

God of life, I pray that you give me greater awareness of your presence in the world around me. Open my eyes and ears to your sights and sounds, so that I may submit to your will my desire to determine what is best for me. I pray that as I learn to consider what honors you most, I might discover how you are igniting the life you are giving me. Let my light shine for Jesus. Amen.

Olympia Presbytery

Washington

As they looked around the room, everyone quickly assessed the face of every other person. Some were old friends, some nearly strangers. All had one thing in common: they had agreed to serve on the Council of the Presbytery of Olympia. They were an interesting mix: young and old, rural and urban, from big churches and small churches, those loving hymns and those into drums. There were conservatives and liberals and progressives and those refusing to accept a title. There were only a few from minority racial ethnic backgrounds but more than there used to be. Some had served the presbytery for years and some were attending their first meeting ever. All were wondering how this crew would ever gel in order to face the challenges of this rapidly changing, foundation-shaking time.

The new moderator raised her voice to begin the opening devotions, inviting everyone to share a brief story of their own baptism, of the day they received the blessed water on their brow that announced God's miracle of love in their lives. As soon as the invitation came, people's expressions changed—there were smiles, faraway looks, twinkling eyes. Then came the stories, flowing out of believers' hearts like living water. "I can't remember a thing, but I've always known I was loved by God." "I was eight or nine. I shouted 'more water' but my mom shushed me!" "I was baptized twice. I know that's wrong but it was wonderful the second time, and I remember it like yesterday." The stories went on, each one bringing smiles of recognition or nods of understanding, or an occasional "Aha" as histories of God's involvement with family continued. Everyone drank from the common well of baptism and felt refreshed.

The Council will face challenges around resources, controversies, risk, and change. But these members will not thirst, and together they will walk into newness of life.

Olympia Presbytery and its 50 churches serve 10,330 members.

Prayer

Dear God, thank you for the waters of baptism that remind us of your presence with us always. Open our eyes this day to see your face in all people. In the name of Jesus. Amen.

Let us join in prayer for:

Presbytery Staff
Rev. Lynn Longfield, general presbyter
Elder Tony Cook, stated clerk/communications
Susie Zych, executive assistant
Crystal Bailey, receptionist/office secretary
Stephen Klump, treasurer
Nathan Young, webmaster

PC(USA) General Assembly Staff
David Dobson, PPC
Stephen Dominski, BOP
Annette Donald, BOP

Daily Lectionary
☼ Ps. 119:73–80, 145 ☾ Ps. 121, 6
Gen. 49:1–28
1 Cor. 10:14—11:1; Mark 7:24–37

Let us join in prayer for:

Elder Steve Aeschbacher,
member, GAMC

Presbytery Staff
Rev. Scott Lumsden, executive presbyter
Rev. Dennis Hughes, stated clerk
Elder Barbara Ranta, associate
stated clerk
Joan Hill, bookkeeper
Mansour Khajehpour, coordinator
of mission and stewardship
Aaron Willett, e-News

PC(USA) General Assembly Staff
Jeff Dorris, GAMC
Mary Douglass, BOP

Seattle Presbytery

Washington

With God's love, two pals from Lake City Presbyterian Church (LCPC) have created an award-winning program that annually serves over 40,000 meals and manages nearly 8,000 volunteer hours. The Hunger Intervention Program (HIP) serves breakfast to homeless adults every day and is teaching others how to duplicate its success.

Marvin Walker and Linda Berger are important to the success of Seattle's Hunger Intervention Program.

HIP began in 1998 with a grant from the Boeing Employees Fund that was given to Operation: Sack Lunch (OSL) to begin a satellite program at LCPC. A group of church friends used the grant and their own donations to assemble the lunches. Linda Berger, former board chair of OSL and the driving force behind the program, transported and served the lunches in downtown Seattle every Friday. Marvin Walker, an appreciative recipient, appeared early as Linda's one-man security force.

By the winter of 2005, other organizations that also fed the homeless were forced to close. LCPC regrouped and began serving lunches three times a week. Linda's friend Rhoda Morrow, experienced in regulatory issues and grant writing, put a structured program in place to obtain free food from other sources and convinced the LCPC Session to provide emergency funding.

In August 2005 HIP was chartered. It had an advisory board, agency status, and a grant from the Presbyterian Hunger Program. HIP now delivers and serves breakfast to as many as two hundred shelter residents every day. Its 110 volunteers include developmentally disabled adults who package meal components. Linda was given the 2007 Mayor's End Hunger Award, and Rhoda has developed a reference manual for organizations interested in developing similar programs.

Seattle Presbytery is blessed with 20,934 members in 55 congregations.

Prayer

Thank you, Lord Jesus, for sustaining us even when times are tough. We pray that you will continue to bless those who serve in your name. Let them be a light in darkness and a sign of hope that leads to you. Amen.

Daily Lectionary
☼ Ps. 34, 146 ☾ Ps. 25, 91
Gen. 49:29—50:14
1 Cor. 11:2–34; Mark 8:1–10

The Presbytery of Yukon

Alaska

The moment was filled with grace. By a unanimous vote the Presbytery of Yukon decided on the spot to establish a partnership relationship with Tayal Presbytery of Taiwan.

It had begun with an earlier visit by the Rev. Nathan Lim, now pastor of Anchor Presbyterian Church, a native Alaskan congregation in Anchorage, to take part in the Taiwanese Presbyterian Church's 150th anniversary celebration. Tayal Presbytery serves the indigenous Atayal tribe. As part of its mission and outreach, Tayal looks for partnerships with other aboriginal groups seeking to be true to Christ while embodying an indigenous form of the Christian faith.

In the winter of 2008 the Rev. Curt Karns, Yukon's executive presbyter, and Elder Rodney Ungwiluk of Gambell Presbyterian Church traveled with the Rev. Lim to Taiwan for visits with members and leaders of Tayal Presbytery. The visits opened up both challenging and promising prospects of partnership. The spiritual health of the Tayal churches and the challenges that they share with the native Alaskan churches were of special interest to the Yukon visitors.

In January 2009 Tayal Presbytery voted to enter into a partnership with the Presbytery of Yukon, and Yukon immediately made plans for a reciprocal visit from Tayal. Elders Utux Lbak and Yumin Hayun flew to Alaska, visited several Native communities, and subsequently met jointly with representatives of the Ahmaogak-Akootchook Memorial Parish and Aywaan Parish. At this meeting both parishes voted to recommend that the Presbytery of Yukon enter into a partnership with Tayal Presbytery.

Utux Lbak and Yumin Hayun were introduced to the full Presbytery of Yukon at its spring meeting in February 2009. Speaking in Mandarin (with Nathan Lim translating), they told of their travels up north and out west and then sang a traditional Atayal welcome song. The presbytery responded joyfully, and it was clear to all that the relationship between the presbyteries had reached the fullness of God's time.

The Presbytery of Yukon ministers with its 23 churches and 2,653 members.

Prayer

God of all that is and will be, we thank you for this witness to the unity of all peoples in your grace. We ask your blessing on this new community of fellowship between the Tayan and Yukon presbyteries, knowing in faith that you will continue to guide and bless this work done in your name. Amen.

Let us join in prayer for:

Presbytery Staff
Rev. Curt Karns, executive presbyter
Jan Burger, administrative assistant
Sharon Rayt, stated clerk
Mary Kron, treasurer
Rev. Leisa Carrick, moderator
Elder Mark Wartes, moderator elect

PC(USA) General Assembly Staff
Thomas Dragani, BOP
Edward Driscoll, BOP

Daily Lectionary
☼ Ps. 5, 147:1–11 ☾ Ps. 27, 51
Gen. 50:15–26
1 Cor. 12:1–11; Mark 8:11–26

The Synod of the Covenant

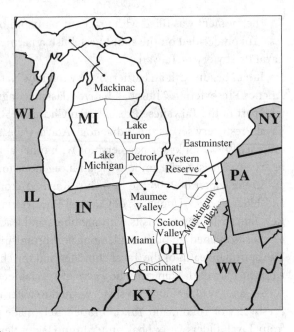

With more than 250 rivers and 155 lakes and bound on the north by four Great Lakes, waters course through the Synod of the Covenant. Even the mighty Ohio River is crossed to include parts of northern Kentucky within the synod, which is made up of 174,284 members in 782 congregations.

Local and international commerce depend on its waterways, as do recreation and tourism. The synod's weather systems are affected by the Great Lakes, and the weather, in turn, affects the smaller lakes and streams. In particular, southeast and northwest Ohio have received the benefits of Presbyterian Disaster Assistance (PDA). The Presbytery of Maumee Valley continues to work with PDA around Findlay, where flooding has caused devastation.

Growing awareness of threats to water sources and a commitment to the stewardship of all creation have motivated many Presbyterians to become involved in preservation. Teams of young people, children, and adults are cleaning up river banks. Others have become involved in local politics. Covenant's seven camps and conference centers and church school programs are including lessons for all ages about caring for God's world.

Daily Lectionary
☼ Ps. 27, 147:12–20 ☾ Ps. 126, 102
Exod. 1:6–22
1 Cor. 12:12–26; Mark 8:27—9:1

Prayer
God of all creation, we give thanks for the day-to-day blessings of clean water and the life it brings forth and sustains. Help us remember to care for your world as we enjoy it. Amen.

The Presbytery of Cincinnati

Indiana, Kentucky, Ohio

When Mt. Washington Presbyterian Church organized a disaster relief trip to the Gulf Coast in November 2005, the after effects of Katrina were still national news. As the congregation planned a return trip, elder David Legg pondered the possibility of a presbytery-wide effort. A former moderator of the Presbytery of Cincinnati, David was personally acquainted with many of the 84 congregations spanning three states, and he felt a calling to extend an invitation to the 16,195 members of the presbytery.

Mission volunteers accept a higher calling.

As a result the second disaster relief trip to the Gulf Coast included workers from several congregations who brought additional gifts to the mission and offered opportunities to create new friendships. Under David Legg's enthusiastic leadership, the mission trips to the Gulf Coast have settled into a twice-a-year event, gathering workers from diverse walks of life to repair homes and offer encouragement to struggling families.

As of this writing eight mission teams have served, and a ninth trip is in the planning stage. David reports that twenty-five congregations, more than a quarter of the churches in the presbytery, have taken part. Well above 10,000 volunteer hours have been invested in repair and rebuilding for people in need.

Asked about memorable moments, David recalls the homeowner who insisted on feeding the team. "It was the best jambalaya I ever tasted," David reports. Growing more serious, he adds, "The faith of the people we've worked with is so strong, and they are so appreciative of our help. No one walks away from one of these trips without knowing we've done something worthwhile."

Prayer

God without boundaries, we praise you for the opportunity to serve neighbors who do not live next door. In Jesus' name, we give thanks for gifts to share, for willing workers, and for the powerful witness of those who meet hardship with faith and affliction with hope. Amen.

Friday, March 19

Let us join in prayer for:

Presbytery Staff
Rev. Jim DiEgidio, general presbyter
Elder Janis Alling Adams, stated clerk, resource coordinator/webmaker
Sandy Phillips, administration and finance coordinator
Marion Montefiore, administrative assistant
Donna Burckle, bookkeeper
George Hufford, hunger, health, and housing concerns coordinator

PC(USA) General Assembly Staff
Diane Dulaney, GAMC
Nancy Lynn Dwyer, BOP
Amelia Dye, BOP

Daily Lectionary
☼ Ps. 22, 148 ☾ Ps. 105, 130
Exod. 2:1–22
1 Cor. 12:27—13:3; Mark 9:2–13

Daily Lectionary
☼ Ps. 43, 149 ☾ Ps. 31, 143
Exod. 2:23—3:15
1 Cor. 13:1–13; Mark 9:14–29

The Presbytery of Detroit

Michigan

The rivers of life are revitalizing Detroit's Woodward Corridor. With the relocation of corporate offices from the suburbs to downtown, new housing is being built next to old. Rich and poor are neighbors.

Into that mix Riverside, an emergent, missional new church development, brings God's word to those with little church background. Weekly worship ends

with the charge, "As you have been fed by the word of God, go and feed those that hunger on the streets of our community." Departing worshipers pick up sack lunches to distribute to those living on the streets just outside the door.

One young worshiper, who himself counted among the hungry, took a sack to an older man on the street. The man in turn gave him a bottle of the water that he sold to survive. The younger man was so moved by this encounter of hunger and thirst being mutually met that he returned, saying, "If this is what you are going to do every week, I am in!"

A father and son worship at Riverside New Church Development in downtown Detroit.

The Rev. Brenda Jarvis, organizing pastor, will build on the probe she directed. Charon Barconey staffs outreach to students and faculty at nearby Wayne State University, inviting them to Riverside's coffeehouse atmosphere with weekday offerings of Bible study and meditative yoga. A mission emphasis being developed is a place of refuge for young men who have aged out of foster care.

Riverside is a river of life streaming in downtown Detroit.

The Presbytery of Detroit is the home of 86 churches with 32,991 members, 3 fellowships, and 2 new church developments.

Prayer

God from whom all water flows, pour your Spirit on the life-giving ministry of Riverside. Strengthen those who bring your word to the streets of Detroit and all cities on this earth. May the day come soon when there are no more rich and poor, satisfied and hungry, but all are one. Amen.

The Lord's Day

Minute for Mission
University of Dubuque Theological Seminary

The Iowa location of the University of Dubuque Theological Seminary provides many opportunities for students to minister in small-town and rural settings.

Members and friends gather in front of the First Presbyterian Church building.

"Living water" in Onslow, Iowa, looks like a new $700 projector, the latest symbol of the new relationships between First Presbyterian Church and its neighbors. Family movie nights with free popcorn are on the church's summer schedule in this farming community of 223.

Changes in the rural economy are reflected in Onslow's slow, long-term decline. First Presbyterian's statistics parallel community trends. "There are no children in our church except for the student pastor's two boys," read the Christian Education Committee's Annual Report in 2008. But now, plans are being made to reestablish Sunday school.

The Spirit has brought blessings of energy and hope as church members are seeing beyond the front doors of the building to envision Christ's call to mission. The dual emphases on mission and relationships come naturally for Dubuque Seminary student Christopher Doyle, a former PC(USA) mission co-worker, and his wife, Hala, a citizen of Palestine. First Presbyterian has hosted a series of mission co-workers and other guests from China, Kenya, and Ukraine. Internal relationships have deepened; awareness of the breadth of God's kingdom has expanded. An elder remarked, "We still have a way to go, but this year has lifted our sagging spirits."

—*Rev. Hal Murry, director of field education,*
University of Dubuque Theological Seminary

Prayer

We look to you, O God, whom we do not see, to renew all that we do see. Train our eyes to see what is to be seen in Christ—new life from the dead, fresh hope from the grave, divine love transforming human emptiness. Amen.

Sunday Lectionary and Hymns

Isa. 43:16–21
The Church's One Foundation
PH 442, HB 437

Ps. 126
When God Delivered Israel
PH 237

Phil. 3:4b–14
Be Thou My Vision
PH 339, HB 303

John 12:1–8
When I Survey the Wondrous Cross
PH 100, 101, HB 198

Daily Lectionary

☼ Ps. 84, 150 ☾ Ps. 42, 32
Exod. 3:16—4:12
Rom. 12:1–21; John 8:46–59

Daily Lectionary
☼ Ps. 119:73–80, 145 ☾ Ps. 121, 6
Exod. 4:10–20 (21–26) 27–31
1 Cor. 14:1–19; Mark 9:30–41

Eastminster Presbytery

Ohio

When Common Ground Church Community in North Lima, Ohio, was chartered by Eastminster Presbytery in 2005, it was worshiping in a high school auditorium. When a nearby nursery and garden center was put up for sale, a vision began to develop. As congregation members looked at the greenhouses, warehouses, garden space, twenty acres of woods, and a showroom that could be converted into worship space, they asked themselves, "What kind of mission might God want us to be involved in?" Located twenty minutes from Youngstown, which had the highest poverty rate in the country for a city its size, the needs were many.

What has emerged is "Goodness Grows." Even before they could worship in their new facility, Common Ground hired an expert in urban agriculture and three college interns, and partnered with a faith-based organization in Youngstown that works with inner-city youth. The youth worked at the site with the youth of the church, and Common Ground explored sites for urban agriculture in the inner city.

Goodness Grows is developing as an urban agricultural ministry training site that teaches about small-scale sustainable agriculture and about microenterprises.

Youth from Common Ground and inner-city youth celebrate the fruits of their labor.

It is continuing its ministry with college interns. Pastor Steve Fortenberry says, "Our three college interns from last summer all found their experience both faith formational and influential upon their discernment of Christian vocation."

Eastminster Presbytery is comprised of 54 congregations with 10,295 members and has within its bounds Joseph Badger Meadows Camp and Conference Center, along with the Presbyterian retirement communities of Park Vista, Lake Vista, and Rockynol.

Prayer
Gracious Lord, thank you for church communities like Common Ground and missions like Goodness Grows, through which you declare the good news of Jesus Christ and bear fruit for your kingdom. Amen.

The Presbytery of Lake Huron

Michigan

Against many odds, Korean American Presbyterian (KAP) Church of the Bible in Grand Blanc, Michigan, is a witness to the faithfulness and might of the almighty God. It was a traumatized congregation when the Rev. Young Kwon arrived four years ago. Most of the twenty-eight members were of retirement age. In the spring of 2008 the church faced the maturation of a five-year balloon mortgage loan. After consultation with the presbytery, it appeared that merging or nesting with another church were its only choices. Even in a tightening credit market, with God's help, KAP received a ten-year commercial loan. Another miracle was the arrival of unsolicited donations from out-of-state donors that amounted to a quarter of its annual budget. KAP also received a grant from the Synod of the Covenant for a creative new ministry effort titled "Hospitality to Asian Exchange Students, University of Michigan, Flint." Now about ten college students regularly attend church.

Members of the Korean American Presbyterian Church of the Bible gather in the church sanctuary.

At the end of 2008 KAP Church ordained new European American elders and deacons, so its officers are now about half Korean and half European Americans. Church membership is truly bicultural and bilingual. Most of the members are blue-collar workers who were not regular church attendees in the past. Through fervent prayer and its best efforts, KAP Church is now able to spend 10 percent of its monthly income for mission.

The Presbytery of Lake Huron has 50 churches, 11,047 members, and includes Alma College within its bounds.

Prayer

Awesome God, you continue to surprise us with your awesome providence. Forgive our incessant unbelief. We thank and love you. With you we cannot fail. Grant that we meet the challenges of this day in you. Give us inner peace that we may see your hand holding us. Amen.

Tuesday, March 23

Let us join in prayer for:

Tim Clark, member, GAMC
Rev. Melissa Derosia, member, GAMC
Rev. Matthew Schramm, member, GAMC

Presbytery Staff
Rev. Louise Brokaw, general presbyter
Rev. Dr. Douglas Tracy, stated clerk
Andrea Drapp, business manager/treasurer
Marquietta Davis, administrative assistant
Staci Percy, communications manager/recording clerk

PC(USA) General Assembly Staff
Elder Joe Edmiston, GAMC
Laura Edwards, FDN

Daily Lectionary
✿ Ps. 34, 146 ☾ Ps. 25, 91
Exod. 5:1—6:1
1 Cor. 14:20–33a, 39–40
Mark 9:42–50

Let us join in prayer for:

Presbytery Staff
John Best, general presbyter
Leslie Keusch, acting office administrator
Richard Lichti, associate presbyter
Janet Magennis, stated clerk
Jane McGookey,
communications consultant
Nancy Maleitzke, office administrator
Larry Nelson, treasurer

PC(USA) General Assembly Staff
Marla Edwards, GAMC
David Eicher, PPC
Vanessa Elkin, FDN

The Presbytery of Lake Michigan

Michigan

The Presbytery of Lake Michigan is a Christian community of congregations and clergy partnering in mission as they "Seek God's Leading, Share God's Love, and Spread God's Light." The presbytery has 16,860 members in 70 churches and an outdoor ministry at Camp Greenwood.

The Global Hosanna Fellowship was founded in March 2005 as a mission branch of John Knox Presbyterian Church in Grand Rapids. The fellowship began as a community of immigrants from Kenya and has expanded to include

Everyone is welcome to line up for dinner on Thursday.

members from Ghana, Sierra Leone, Tanzania, and the Democratic Republic of the Congo. Today this partnership finds expression in a joint youth group, Sunday school, pastoral care, and shared leadership of worship experiences. The Rev. Johnson W. Mwara, ordained by the Presbyterian Church of East Africa and a member of the presbytery, is the pastor of the Global Hosanna Fellowship. The Rev. Michael Baynai is the pastor of John Knox.

The Welcome Home Dinner is a ministry of First Presbyterian of Benton Harbor. Gathering on Thursday evenings, the dinner brings together a wonderful diversity: those on their way home from work, recipients of the church's food bank, retired folks, church folks, and persons recently released from prison. Everyone is included; there is no us, no them. One former inmate said, "Before I came to your church, no one had hugged me in fifteen years." The presbytery partners with First Presbyterian in this ministry.

The presbytery will help host, with ecumenical partnership in the Reformed Church in America and the Christian Reformed Church, the historic Uniting General Council launching the new World Communion of Reformed Churches in Grand Rapids in June 2010.

Daily Lectionary
☼ Ps. 5, 147:1–11 ☾ Ps. 27, 51
Exod. 7:8–24
2 Cor. 2:14—3:6; Mark 10:1–16

Prayer
Gracious God, we thank you for communities of faith, young and old, who find in your will and vision a fresh calling to embody the good news in Christ. Amen.

The Presbytery of Mackinac

Michigan, Wisconsin

The churches in the Presbytery of Mackinac have been encouraged to consider ministries that would provide new vitality to their congregations and their neighborhoods. For the past three years the budget for the presbytery has included monies to support identified mission initiatives that congregations could apply for. These one-time grants of up to $2,000 may be used as start-up funds for new ministries.

The Church of the Straits, a congregation in Mackinaw City, has been serving an aging population that is challenged by the hazards of winter. With technological help, the church developed a Web site that allows those who cannot attend a morning service to hear the sermon online. The worship committee purchased a CD copier so a deacon can take copies of the worship service to the nearby assisted living center. To provide for more effective communication with members, a phone tree system informs members of pastoral and program concerns. The pastor, the Rev. Dave Wallis, is grateful for the grant support that enhanced the ability to reach out to church members, especially the elderly and homebound.

A pastor at St. Andrews Presbyterian in Beulah, Michigan, was aware of young families in a neighboring community who had limited access to resources. Without reliable transportation they used a county bus system to reach agencies that offered assistance. Many of the families, however, could not afford the bus tokens. The Rev. Shelaine Bird asked the presbytery for funds to provide free tokens, which church volunteers now distribute each week at the bus stop at the church parking lot.

As the news of new ministries is shared, other congregations begin to discover new mission possibilities in their own communities. These grants are a reservoir from which flow streams of water that bring life to the many who thirst for the good news.

Mackinac is home to 6,820 members in 41 congregations and Presbytery Point Camp. Its Web site is www.presbymac.org.

Prayer

Creator and creative Lord who makes all things possible, refresh your people with the holy hope of new and fresh beginnings, that we may not give up in difficult times or give in when we are discouraged. May we use the gifts you graciously provide to respond to the thirst of neighbors in need of your saving grace. Amen.

Thursday, March 25

Let us join in prayer for:

Presbytery Staff
Dr. Harry Begley, stated clerk
Lindy Bearss, administrative assistant
Elder Walter Moore, treasurer

PC(USA) General Assembly Staff
Christie Elliott, GAMC
Rev. Bob Ellis, GAMC

Daily Lectionary
☼ Ps. 27, 147:12–20 ☾ Ps. 126, 102
Exod. 7:25—8:19
2 Cor. 3:7–18; Mark 10:17–31

Maumee Valley Presbytery

Ohio, Michigan

When Sunday school teacher Lynn Hunsicker prepared her lesson on what children can do to live their faith by expressing acts of kindness to others, she couldn't have imagined what it would lead to. On the first Sunday her class distributed three comfort pillows in worship. Within a few months church members were making pillows for people in need of hope and comfort. The entire congregation of First Presbyterian in Sandusky, Ohio, was so inspired that the members have made 4,000 pillows for people everywhere.

The comfort pillows carry a message of love and support from the church and are to be passed on whenever possible. The message encourages people to contact their local Presbyterian church if they want to know more about God's love for them. The pillows have gone to children's organizations and to hospice and cancer treatment providers in the Sandusky community. A few church members help area children make the pillows to keep or give to someone they know who needs love and support. On Make a Difference Day the youth of the church delivered over 450 pillows to residents of Ohio Veterans Home.

Church members, community members, and the local Kohl's store worked together to create 43 blankets for homeless people.

Recently, First Presbyterian received grants to make blankets for those in the area without shelter. These comfort blankets carry the message of God's love. Most important, each Sunday the congregation prays for everyone who has received a pillow or blanket from this ministry. In this way the church has taken on the task of putting the needs of others above its own needs. This has been a joyfully transforming experience for the congregation as these Presbyterians deepen their faith by following God's lead in directions they had never expected!

Maumee Valley Presbytery has 76 churches with 11,484 members.

Prayer

O God, you call us, asking us to follow in faith and not knowing where you will lead. Thank you for new ways to share your love and see your Spirit working. May we continue to be in prayer and action for those who need hope and comfort in you. Amen.

The Presbytery of the Miami Valley

Ohio

In June 2007 a mission team from Lebanon Presbyterian Church in southeastern Ohio traveled to Kenya to build a Christian medical clinic. "It seemed like an impossible undertaking, but we felt very strongly that the Lord was calling us to go to Africa," explains pastor Peter Larson.

The clinic was established in partnership with the Presbyterian Church of East Africa in the village of Ng'undu, east of Nairobi. Before the clinic opened, people in the area

The people of Ng'undu have set an ambitious goal of planting one million trees in the area around the medical clinic.

had had to walk up to eighteen miles for medical treatment. The new clinic is housed in an old farmhouse that was completely rebuilt. It is staffed by a registered nurse and laboratory technician. Doctors from Nairobi regularly treat patients who require additional care.

Since the mission team returned from Africa, the Lebanon church has worked with the Presbytery of the Miami Valley to establish the Africa Medical Mission Network, which involves several other congregations. In recent years the presbytery has provided more than $5,000 to help support the clinic, whose annual budget is about $28,000. Financial support also comes from rummage sales held twice a year.

The medical clinic has brought new hope to the people of Ng'undu. The residents recently set an ambitious goal to plant one million trees.

The Africa Medical Mission Network is planning to fund a well-drilling project that would provide water at Ilmamen Presbyterian Church in Mashuru, a drought-stricken region inhabited by the Masai people.

The presbytery has 63 congregations with 13,518 members.

Prayer

By your reconciling love in Jesus Christ, loving God, distance and difference matter none. You have let us touch the hearts of others as our hearts have been touched by them, and we, caressed and nurtured in your love, no longer stay strangers, but grow as friends. Throughout our world, may it ever be so. Amen.

Let us join in prayer for:

Presbytery Staff
Elder Dennis H. Piermont, executive presbyter
Rev. Doris Arnett Whitaker, stated clerk
Thomas F. Oxley III, office manager
Martha Kiel, treasurer
Elder Joyce Routzohn, bookkeeper

PC(USA) General Assembly Staff
Didi Emerson, GAMC
Rev. Emily Enders Odom, GAMC

Daily Lectionary
☼ Ps. 43, 149 ☾ Ps. 31, 143
Exod. 10:21—11:8
2 Cor. 4:13–18; Mark 10:46–52

Sunday Lectionary and Hymns

Luke 19:28–40
All Glory, Laud, and Honor
PH 88, HB 187

Ps. 118:1–2, 19–29
This Is the Day the Lord Hath Made
PH 230, HB 69

Isa. 50:4–9a
O Love, How Deep, How Broad, How High
PH 83

Ps. 31:9–16
PH 182

Phil. 2:5–11
PPCS 186
Ride On! Ride On in Majesty!
PH 90, 91, HB 188

Luke 22:14—23:56
Go to Dark Gethsemane
PH 97, HB 193
or
Luke 23:1–49
O Sacred Head, Now Wounded
PH 98, HB 194

Daily Lectionary
☼ Ps. 84, 150 ☾ Ps. 42, 32
Zech. 9:9–12
1 Tim. 6:12–16 *or* Zech. 12:9–11, 13:1, 7–9; Luke 19:41–48

The Lord's Day
Minute for Mission: Passion/Palm Sunday

Jerusalem was a tough town. Roman rule was harsh. Local authorities were brutal and unmerciful. For the Hebrew people, life was difficult at best and deadly at worst. Living in Jerusalem could feel like living in a prison. Or a graveyard.

And yet, into their lives on that hot, dusty Palm Sunday came one who offered hope. They couldn't have known that five days later he would suffer the same fate as so many of them. No, on this day, the promise of life abundant was on all their minds as Jesus rode into town with his ragtag band of followers. They could not help but rejoice.

This building is the new home for the Moscow Protestant Chaplaincy's African immigrant community center.

African immigrants in Moscow, Russia, also can find life brutal and even deadly. Rampant racism has created a climate in which discrimination and physical violence are a constant threat. For these folk, too, life can feel like a prison. Or a graveyard.

But hope has come to them in the form of another ragtag band of followers of Jesus—members of the PC(USA)-supported Moscow Protestant Chaplaincy. This multiracial, multicultural congregation, pastored by the Rev. Bob Bronkema, has opened its doors to African immigrants, offering legal assistance to those who are attacked and providing a range of social services that offer hope and safety.

Moscow Protestant Chaplaincy has recently found a new home for its growing African immigrant outreach program—an unused building in a cemetery! "It's a perfect location for a ministry that promises resurrection," Bob Bronkema says.

—*Rev. Jerry L. Van Marter, Presbyterian News Service, General Assembly Mission Council*

Prayer
Great God, in Jesus Christ you rescued the world for us. You rescued us. Now lead us, as followers of Jesus, to help rescue others whom you love. We don't have to go to Russia— sisters and brothers right here need the hope and safety promised in the gospel. Help us to be faithful bearers of Christ's hope and peace. Amen.

The Presbytery of Muskingum Valley

Ohio

The Presbytery of Muskingum Valley (MVP) seeks to journey with Jesus to touch the world—empowered by the Spirit to make disciples, nurture the faith, and serve the needs of the community. For MVP, God's missional call is born from hearts that love, listen,

Prayers abound for new pastor Jack McClelland.

and learn in order to touch the world. Staff and congregation members know that deep trust can be built only as relationships are grounded in the authenticity and integrity born of knowing one another in Christ. By incorporating core principles of discipleship they seek to understand the joy and power born of serving in the supply of the Spirit. Heeding God's missional call begins with lives that are grounded in Christ.

Five key principles guide the presbytery's shared mission. As leaders they seek to empower congregations to be the primary agents of mission in their communities and beyond; to seek, respond to, and nurture kairos moments leading to renewed commitment to mission in pastors, leaders, and their congregations; to equip congregations to be communities that make disciples of Jesus by imparting the content, vocabulary, and practices of following Christ through faithful and intentional relationships; to work with governing bodies to direct resources to congregations bearing fruit; and to lay an administrative foundation to undergird and support the mission of making disciples, nurturing their faith, and serving the needs of community.

Presbytery leadership serves as shepherd and servant to its congregations with the understanding that congregations are God's mission outposts in the world. MVP's 11,302 members worship in 93 churches.

Prayer

Lord Christ, take us. Mold us. Change us. Use us—all according to your will and all for your coming realm. Amen.

Let us join in prayer for:

Elder Cathryn C. Piekarski, member, GAMC

Presbytery Staff
Deborah Rundlett, general presbyter
Martin Radcliff, stated clerk
Erin Shilling, administrative assistance
Barbara Schie, financial assistant
Pat Karnosh, office assistant

PC(USA) General Assembly Staff
Rev. Barry Ensign-George, GAMC
Elder Betsy Ensign-George, GAMC
Jeanette Evans, GAMC

Daily Lectionary

☼ Ps. 119:73–80, 145 ☾ Ps. 121, 6
Lam. 1:1–2, 6–12
2 Cor. 1:1–7; Mark 11:12–25

Let us join in prayer for:

Elder Joyce A. Smith, member, GAMC

Presbytery Staff
Dana Knapp, executive presbyter
Jeannie Harsh, associate
executive presbyter
Dagmar Romage, office manager
Brenda Oliver, business manager
Richard Hays, stated clerk

PC(USA) General Assembly Staff
Elder Joyce Evans, OGA
Daniel Fabia, BOP
Michael Fallon, BOP

Daily Lectionary
☼ Ps. 34, 146 ☾ Ps. 25, 91
Lam. 1:17–22
2 Cor. 1:8–22; Mark 11:27–33

The Presbytery of Scioto Valley

Ohio

Jane Gear

BCLC graduate Justin White celebrates his high school graduation.

Believing that learning is inextricably tied to discipleship and the public welfare, the Presbyterian Church (U.S.A.) and its predecessors have had a long history of commitment to education through church operated, supported, and affiliated schools and policy statements on education. Founded in January 2003 Brookwood Presbyterian Church's Brookwood Community Learning Center (BCLC) stands firmly within this Reformed tradition of commitment to educational excellence and justice.

As envisioned by Elder Ellen Wristen, a special needs attorney and advocate, and the Rev. John Birkner, BCLC seeks to provide an alternative educational site and program for students who, as a result of academic challenges, socialization issues, frequent suspensions, or expulsions, would otherwise be served through home instruction, home schooling, or not at all. BCLC's student body consists entirely of students with social or educational challenges such as autism, ADD/ADHD, oppositional defiant disorder, bipolar disorder, or combinations thereof. BCLC provides these students and their families a safe learning environment that fosters healthy peer and adult/student relationships, thus providing a supportive and challenging learning experience in which all children can truly reach their full academic potential.

BCLC, with financial assistance from the Synod of the Covenant, has grown from twenty-four students and four part-time staff to fifty to seventy students and a full-time staff that includes two social workers, two reading specialists, two math specialists, a speech therapist, three special education teachers, sixteen paraprofessionals, and numerous church volunteers. Coupled with the prayers and support of the church, this low student-to-staff ratio has resulted in the vast majority of BCLC's students passing the statewide proficiencies and in several students becoming the first members of their families to attend college.

The Presbytery of Scioto Valley has 113 churches and 21,681 members.

Prayer
Lord, teach us to train children in the way that they should go, so that when they are old they will not depart from it. Amen.

The Presbytery of the Western Reserve

Ohio

The Presbytery of the Western Reserve in northeast Ohio, which encompasses the greater Cleveland metropolitan area, has 49 churches, 2 new church developments, and 11,123 members. It is home to world-class medical and biomedical research facilities that have attracted a growing number of Asian and Asian American doctors and medical students.

A decade ago the Korean Central Presbyterian Church of Greater Cleveland saw the need to develop a distinct English-speaking ministry—called "The Tapestry"—to minister to adult, second-generation Korean Americans. The metaphor emphasizes how the Holy Spirit weaves together individual lives (yarns) to tell the community's story around the Lord's Table. (The folksy explanation is that nearly all Christian Korean Americans growing up in the United States have had a tapestry of da Vinci's *Last Supper* in their homes.)

Pastor Jake Kim and other members of The Tapestry serve dinner at Korean Culture Camp.

Their mission is to serve the growing generation of Asian Americans with the gospel of Jesus Christ. Their mission statement is "To Know God and to Make God Known" as a community of "Joy, Love, and Hope." Since the summer of 2007 the English ministry has tripled in attendance, with an increase in couples in their thirties and forties. This is a growing multiracial/multicultural congregation with a third of its congregation being non-Korean.

Their mission service projects minister to the area's Korean American college and graduate students. They also partner with the Korean-speaking congregation to support Korean Culture Camp of Cleveland, an educational heritage and pride camp for seventy-five children adopted from Korea.

The Tapestry owes its existence to the missional vision, generous funding, and prayers of the Korean Central Presbyterian Church of Greater Cleveland.

Prayer

God, help us better minister and reach out to Asian American young adult singles and nonbelievers with the love and message of Jesus Christ. Amen.

Let us join in prayer for:

Presbytery Staff
Liza Hendricks, general presbyter
Jody LeFort, stated clerk and associate presbyter for equipping leaders
Susan Holderness, pastor to clergy and their families
Laura VanDale, hunger action enabler
Susan Gillespie, staff associate for hospitality and communication
Laurie Steidel, staff associate for finance and data management
Lee Lohr, staff associate to the general presbyter and stated clerk

PC(USA) General Assembly Staff
Margaret Farmer, GAMC
Anthony Farrell, GAMC

Daily Lectionary

☉ Ps. 5, 147:1–11 ☾ Ps. 27, 51
Lam. 2:1–9
2 Cor. 1:23—2:11; Mark 12:1–11

Maundy Thursday

Minute for Mission

As a child growing up in Vermont Avenue Presbyterian Church (now Community United Presbyterian Church) in Los Angeles, California, I was always fascinated by Communion. Every first Sunday I could only dream of partaking of the elements because I was not of age, not to mention my aunt's admonition to my two brothers and me that we needed to understand the meaning and significance. When I was finally allowed to receive Communion, I noticed that some people would let the bread and wine pass them by. One time I was so perplexed by someone's refusal to take Communion that I summoned up courage and asked, "Why are you not taking Communion?" The person replied, "I examined myself and found that I did not deserve Communion today."

In 1 Corinthians 11:27–32, Paul speaks to the Corinthian community, which was struggling with many issues, including the Lord's Supper. He writes, "Examine yourselves" and then eat of the bread and drink of the cup.

On this holy night of Maundy Thursday, we can give thanks to God that Jesus is going to face his final hour on our behalf.

Sometimes as the community of faith we are called to self-examination. We have not always followed in the ways of Jesus Christ, individually or as a community. Undoubtedly we feel unworthy at times of participating in the Lord's Supper. Let us do as Paul advises—examine ourselves and then eat of the bread and drink of the cup. On this holy night of Maundy Thursday, we can give thanks to God that Jesus is going to face his final hour on our behalf. It is through the grace of God and through the son Jesus that we are able to live, breathe, and have our being in spite of our shortcomings. May we remember this as we journey to Calvary!

—*Rev. Dr. Byron Wade, vice-moderator,*
218th General Assembly of the Presbyterian Church (U.S.A.) (2008)

Prayer

Holy God, we thank you for your son Jesus on this night. As we prepare to partake of Communion, help us to examine ourselves and rest in the assurance that although we have fallen short of following your ways, it is through Jesus' life, death, and resurrection that we are able to live for and serve you. In the name of Christ we pray. Amen.

Daily Lectionary
☼ Ps. 27, 147:12–20 ☾ Ps. 126, 102
Lam. 2:10–18
1 Cor. 10:14–17, 11:27–32
Mark 14:12–25

Good Friday

Minute for Mission

One of the most vivid images associated with Good Friday is the image of darkness. Three of the four Gospels speak of the darkness that accompanied the crucifixion. Darkness conjures up an ominous image that easily elicits emotions like fear and dread. The wonderful thing about the story of Christ is that it neither dwells on nor concludes with the theme of darkness because, thanks be to God, darkness is highly susceptible to light. Indeed, the darkness of the crucifixion is utterly shattered by the light of Jesus' resurrection, and as a result, the power of darkness is lost, lost in the redeeming light of God's love.

Several years ago while serving on the PC(USA)'s Self-Development of People Committee, I learned firsthand about the magnitude of darkness in our world. I learned about the murder and intimidation the Guatemalan people faced at a dark moment in their history; I learned about the darkness that encompassed the people of South Carolina's Sea Islands, where the descendants of former slaves struggled to maintain dignity and sustenance in the face of the powerful forces of encroaching development; I learned about the darkness of displacement as urban dwellers fought to hold on to a place to live in the face of rising costs and growing homelessness.

> *Thanks be to God, darkness is highly susceptible to light.*

Miraculously, the powers of darkness did not overcome the spirit of the people in these situations. Their knowledge of the resurrection infused them with strength and hope, and the church, through its mission, helped fuel the light that broke the darkness in their lives. Mission is a vital element of the light the church brings to a world frequently immersed in darkness; it is the church's active response to the initiative God takes in the death and resurrection of Jesus.

—*Rev. Curtis A. Kearns, Jr., executive administrator,*
General Assembly Mission Council

Prayer

Gracious God, your light fills us with joy and hope. Help us to be joyful and hopeful in our witness. Your light overcomes fear and dread. Help us to resist fearfulness and dreariness so that we live with the confidence of resurrection people. O God, help us to fuel the light that saves the world. Amen.

Daily Lectionary

☼ Ps. 22, 148 ☾ Ps. 105, 130
Lam. 3:1–9, 19–33
1 Peter 1:10–20
John 13:36–38 *or* John 19:38–42

The Synod of Lakes and Prairies

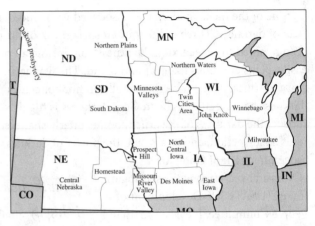

Hillcrest Family Services of Dubuque, Iowa, a ministry partner of the Synod of Lakes and Prairies, is committed to form "promise people" by striving to fulfill six promises relating to caring adults, safe places, healthy starts, effective education, an opportunity for service, and an opportunity for a spiritual conversation.

One mother and father wrote about their son's experience at Hillcrest. "We left him there a scared, confused, depressed, angry, and lost teenage boy. As the days turned into weeks and then months, we got to know many of you better, and you became like family. Our son lived with people who truly cared about and respected him, who set high standards and held him accountable, who provided him with opportunities to learn, work, and serve others, and who wanted to see him experience success and happiness as much as we did. We are very proud of the young man that he has become and thank you for the special role each of you played in that." In a typical year Hillcrest serves more than 20,000 people in Iowa through twenty-three programs and at thirteen sites.

The synod includes 908 churches with 154,623 members. It has covenant relationships with seven Presbyterian institutions of higher education—Buena Vista University, Carroll University, Coe College, Hastings College, Jamestown College, Macalester College, and the University of Dubuque and the University of Dubuque Theological Seminary.

Prayer

God of mercy, forgive our tendency to place limits on your grace. Help us recognize your invitation to quench our thirst with the living water you offer. Let us celebrate this day and every day the everlasting life we have in Jesus Christ. Amen.

Daily Lectionary

☼ Ps. 43, 149 ☽ Ps. 31, 143
Lam. 3:37–58
Heb. 4:1–16; Rom. 8:1–11

The Lord's Day

Minute for Mission: One Great Hour of Sharing/Easter

Christ's last words to his disciples in John's Gospel are, "Do you love me? Feed my sheep . . . follow me." Although he knew their answer, Jesus three times asked them, "Do you love me?" Each time that the disciples respond "Of course we do," Jesus tells them to tend his flock, to care for those he loves. They're just beginning to understand what this implies: Live your love for me by tending these for whom I have sacrificed everything; give food to the hungry, clean water to the thirsty, clothing to the naked, health care to the sick; welcome the refugee and the stranger; share your strength and refuge with the fearful; rescue those in danger; bring justice to the oppressed.

Only by sharing God's love can you fully open yourself to it.

A tall order then as today—more than anyone can take on alone. But when we work together with millions of other disciples through One Great Hour of Sharing, such impossible demands start to seem realistic. Change begins to happen.

It is not just for the world's poor and oppressed that Jesus instructs his disciples to feed his sheep. His whole life proclaims the deep paradox that only by giving up what is most valuable to you can you make it yours. Only by sharing God's love can you fully open yourself to it. Only by letting go your attachment to security can you find the security that comes from trusting God. Thus his commandment is also an invitation to transformation.

The same invitation is extended to us. Our gifts to One Great Hour of Sharing offer us a way to joyfully accept that invitation. Tending Christ's sheep, we can help open both the world and our own lives to the transforming love of God. Let us give generously.

—*Elder Alan Krome, associate for special offerings, General Assembly Mission Council*

Prayer

Dear God, you continually invite us to be part of your transformation of the world, but we often have other things to take care of first. Help us recognize that nothing in our lives is more important, more meaningful, more transformative than to accept Christ's invitation to feed his sheep. Accept our gifts, and grant that we may take some part in changing the lives of your beloved children. We ask this in the name of your risen Son. Amen.

Sunday Lectionary and Hymns

Acts 10:34–43
Alleluia, Alleluia! Give Thanks
PH 106
or
Isa. 65:17–25
Christ Is Risen! Shout Hosanna!
PH 104

Ps. 118:1–2, 14–24
PH 231
The Glorious Gates of Righteousness
HB 71

1 Cor. 15:19–26
or
Acts 10:34–43
Because You Live, O Christ
PH 105

John 20:1–18
Jesus Christ Is Risen Today
PH 123, HB 204
or
Luke 24:1–12
Celebrate with Joy and Singing
PH 107

Daily Lectionary

☉ Ps. 93, 150 ☾ Ps. 136, 117
Exod. 12:1–14
John 1:1–18 *or* Isa. 51:9–11
Luke 24:13–35 *or* John 20:19–23

Monday, April 5

Let us join in prayer for:

Presbytery Staff
Rev. Robert Houser, general presbyter
Angela Palmer, office manager

PC(USA) General Assembly Staff
Julie Florence, GAMC
Rob Fohr, GAMC
Sarah Foreman, PPC

The Presbytery of Central Nebraska

Lexington, a community in the Presbytery of Central Nebraska, has a majority racial ethnic population. In recent years the immigration of Latino, Somali, Eastern European, and Sudanese people has increased.

The congregation of First Presbyterian Church in Grand Island helped resettle Laotian refugees many years ago. A worshiping fellowship of forty Sudanese (Nuer) people now share its chapel. The fellowship meets separately for worship in their native language, and their children participate in the Wednesday Logos program and mission trips. A few immigrants worship with the Anglo congregation on Sunday morning. In December 2008 seven of the children were baptized.

Children from First Presbyterian, Grand Island, share mission and friendship.

Late in 2008 pastors working with Sudanese immigrants met to discuss the challenges presented by this new ministry and mission. English as a second language, pastoral leadership, cultural adjustments (especially around parenting issues), and housing and financial issues were a few that were addressed. Questions arose about authorization and registration of baptisms, membership of the parents, and whether they should be listed on church rolls. Temporary solutions have been created, but more discussion will be needed in the future among the fellowship, the session, and the presbytery.

The Sudanese fellowship network crosses presbytery boundaries in Nebraska, but the presbytery lacks a comparable network. It is both interesting and vexing to be in the position of wanting to be helpful and not knowing for sure what will help most.

The Presbytery of Central Nebraska has 41 congregations with 4,895 members. Hastings College is within its bounds.

Prayer

Gracious and merciful Lord God, as you bring us people you love from all over the world, give us hearts to love, care, and share in ministry. Help us to remember that at some point in their lives your people have found themselves to be strangers in a new land. May we learn to welcome as you have welcomed all of your people. In Jesus' name we pray. Amen.

Daily Lectionary
☼ Ps. 97, 145 ☾ Ps. 124, 115
Exod. 12:14–27
1 Cor. 15:1–11; Mark 16:1–8

The Presbytery of Dakota

Nongeographic

Presbyterian youth and young adults often visit the 21 churches with 914 members of the Presbytery of Dakota to extend the gift of living water to the people. But those who have gone to minister frequently find themselves the recipients of the larger portion of God's gifts and often leave feeling that they received more than they gave.

The Rev. Mary Holtey, associate pastor for congregational nurture at First Presbyterian in Fargo, North Dakota, described her church's relationship with the congregations of the presbytery in the following letter:

"Perhaps the most significant and ongoing relationship is with Bdecan Presbyterian Church, Tokio, North Dakota, the only Dakota church within the geographical bounds of the Presbytery of the Northern Plains. Many congregations within our presbytery have maintained supportive and caring relationships with the people of Bdecan by worshiping together; sharing meals, Communion, and baptism; joining youth groups; having rummage and bake sales; and constructing and celebrating their new church building and grounds. These have been and continue to be very meaningful, profound friendships.

"In addition to Bdecan, the Fargo church has traveled to Fraser and Wolf Point, Montana, on two occasions and once to Oglala, South Dakota, to conduct weeklong vacation Bible schools. We would start the week with an expected number of children and by the end of the week it would be tripled with additional friends and family.

"On all these occasions we begin with the intent of bringing the love of Jesus Christ to these communities, and by the end of our visit we would feel like the ones being ministered to, having received so much more from our experiences than we feel we gave.

"The volunteers have felt enriched by these experiences with the people of the presbytery and through the friendships we have made in these congregations and communities. Thank you for these opportunities to share in the ministry of Jesus Christ and to the service of the people of God."

Prayer

Most loving God, who provides the image of pure, living water as the source for all life, we worship you and thank you for your mercy and grace. Guide our feet as we move through this life, knowing that only you provide the gift of eternal life. We pray in the name of Jesus Christ. Amen.

Let us join in prayer for:

Presbytery Staff
Rev. Simon Looking Elk, stated clerk

PC(USA) General Assembly Staff
Quinn Fox, GAMC
Penny Franklin, GAMC

Daily Lectionary

☼ Ps. 98, 146 ☾ Ps. 66, 116
Exod. 12:28–39
1 Cor. 15:12–28; Mark 16:9–20

Daily Lectionary
☼ Ps. 99, 147:1–11 ☾ Ps. 9, 118
Exod. 12:40–51
1 Cor. 15:(29) 30–41; Matt. 28:1–16

The Presbytery of Des Moines

Iowa

Since 1990 a joint ecumenical mission of the Presbytery of Des Moines and Our Sister Parish has been helping the communities of Berlin, El Salvador, break through poverty. This work in progress includes Presbyterian, Disciples of Christ, Catholic, and United Methodist churches.

A family in El Recreo now has clean water.

Compañeros, the presbytery's mission team, partnered with Rotary International in the United States and El Salvador to manufacture and install slow sand water filters in households, providing a sustainable source of safe drinking water to all. The simplicity of the filters makes them ideal for homes scattered over the mountainside: pour water in, let gravity and nature take their course, and soon there is clean drinking water. No electricity, chemicals, or moving parts are required (see www.oursisterparish.org) and, properly used, a filter can last for decades.

The process starts with testing local water sources to confirm the filters will work. Not everything can be removed (like arsenic or heavy metal contamination). However, bacteria and parasites are the main issue with the streams, springs, and rainwater collection tanks that provide water for almost everyone in Berlin. Kathy Mahler, presbytery-designated mission worker, feels lucky to see the process firsthand. The filtered water usually retests at 99 percent bacteria- and parasite-free.

"Hope is such a powerful thing," acknowledges Kathy. "And action by those with good hearts and willing bodies and spirits to carry out the necessary work is priceless."

The Presbytery of Des Moines has 63 congregations, with 9,180 members. To learn more, go to www.presbyteryofdesmoines.org.

Prayer

O God, pour out on us the water of life to all who thirst. We lift up those who walk hours to distant streams, who kneel beside rivers and ponds to drink, cook, and wash. We lift up those for whom clean water is a luxury. Let there be clean water for all who lack what we take for granted. Amen.

The Presbytery of East Iowa

The Presbytery of East Iowa (PEIA) extends 168 miles from north to south following the paths of the Wapsipinicon, Cedar, and Iowa rivers that converge into the mighty Mississippi. During the summer of 2008, nearly all the communities along these rivers experienced flooding. On June 13, 2008, the presbytery office mobilized and became a disaster recovery site. The task would have been overwhelming without the outpouring of God's love both within the presbytery and the greater PC(USA).

The connectional church in action was demonstrated as story after story unfolded. A truckload of generators, wet/dry vacuum cleaners, and supplies arrived from New York. PEIA's sister Presbytery of Ceará in Fortaleza, Brazil, sent money for flood relief. The presbytery received more than $58,000 in outside donations. Lend A Hand, a mission of the Presbytery of Carlisle, sent work teams to Oakville. Presbyterian churches from coast to coast sent volunteers. The Presbyterian Disaster Assistance (PDA) call center coordinated accommodations.

Almost half of PEIA congregations have worked on flood relief and have sent $50,000 in contributions. Four churches are serving as hospitality sites: Christ Church and Westminster in Cedar Rapids, St. Andrew in Iowa City, and Oakville United Methodist. With financial help from PDA, they have housed 332 volunteer work teams from 29 states logging 11,388 worker days and 83,040 hours.

Volunteers from Heartland Presbyterian in Clive, Iowa, worked to repair this flood-damaged home in Cedar Rapids.

PEIA churches have helped with such flood-related ministries as work teams; immediate shelter and supplies; gifts, snack bags, meals, and housing; shower facilities; and thank-you notes and posters.

The 79 churches in the presbytery serve 15,040 members. Within East Iowa's bounds are Camp Wyoming, a mission of the presbytery, and Presbyterian-related Coe College.

Prayer

Lord, you called Noah and his family to serve you in the flood. Help each of us to hear your call. Stir up your power and enable us to serve in ways great and small. Amen.

Thursday, April 8

Let us join in prayer for:

Presbytery Staff
Elder Harry D. Olthoff, general presbyter/facilitator
Dr. Rebecca S. Blair, stated clerk
Rev. Maurie Campbell, education consultant
Sarah Dyck, coordinator for disaster recovery
Rev. John H. Hougen, dean, CLP program
Elder Harry G. Hoyt, committee on ministry consultant
Elder Karen M. Minnis, CLP, visioning consultant
Pamela S. Prather, administrative assistant/finance
Rev. Colette Ciha Soults, worship consultant
Dr. Richard P. Tiegs, administrative assistant
Elder David Van Dusseldorp, treasurer
Marue White, associate for communications

PC(USA) General Assembly Staff
Wanda Fuller, APCU
Jennifer Furjanic, BOP

Daily Lectionary

☼ Ps. 47, 147:12–20 ☾ Ps. 68, 113
Exod. 13:3–10
1 Cor. 15:41–50; Matt. 28:16–20

Let us join in prayer for:

Presbytery Staff
Rev. Richard Wyatt, executive presbyter
Rev. Harold Rainey, stated clerk
Elder Willard Bouwens, treasurer
Elder Barbara Hipple, mission and
outreach coordinator
Elder Kris Peterson, communications
and resource coordinator

PC(USA) General Assembly Staff
Bethany Furkin, GAMC
Rosemary Gallagher, BOP
Rev. Marissa Galvan-Valle, GAMC

Homestead Presbytery

Nebraska

Homestead Presbytery underwent a major transition in 2009. It had already gone paperless for meetings and limited its mailings, but early in 2009 the presbytery went completely virtual—meaning everything is accessible through the Web site. There are no stamps, minimal paper, and nothing but the Internet. Even the directory is online. Sixteen file drawers were reduced to three. Only personnel records and church information that must have hard copies still exist, and even that information is accessible via the Web site by those who need it. Once everything was working virtually, the presbytery council voted to make the staff more available to work with the congregations. So, the Homestead staff became field-based—truly working with the people, resourcing the pastors, church committees, and congregational members. No one was in the office to answer the phone or receive the mail, so the staff became decentralized. Each staff member has a home office. The presbytery phone is a cell phone—it goes with the staff wherever they go. A church is providing a room for the resources (mostly curriculum—everything else is online) and provides the presbytery staff with a mailing address. The staff still meets weekly and actually sees each other together more often now than when they were in an office. For those folks who are not friendly with computers, partners have been set up with each congregation to help disseminate information. In another transition, the presbytery welcomed a new executive presbyter.

How has this transition furthered the mission of Homestead Presbytery? It has helped the presbytery be more connectional than ever—sharing resources, sharing technology, sharing information, and sharing the love of God as one body like never before.

The presbytery is home to 56 congregations, 9,732 members, and Calvin Crest Camp and Conference Center.

Prayer

Our Heavenly Father, transition can be so difficult sometimes, but with change comes growth. Please bless the ministry of Homestead Presbytery churches, and help the connectionalism that is growing out of change to be infectious and a blessing to you. Amen.

The Presbytery of John Knox

Iowa, Minnesota, Wisconsin

Known for their "get 'er done" attitude, members of First Presbyterian Church in Cambria, Wisconsin, are quick to roll up their sleeves and help. Along with others from the Presbytery of John Knox, they've sent teams to the Gulf Coast to work with Presbyterian Disaster Assistance (PDA). After floodwaters destroyed communities along the Mississippi, Cambria's youth assembled clean-up buckets, and a contingent of

The crew from First Presbyterian, Cambria, joined PDA in Gulf Coast recovery work.

workers took them to the devastated area—and stayed to help. The Cambria congregation responded to an appeal for warm clothes by a pastor whose Iowa community faced an unprecedented influx of immigrants. In ten days, eight congregations gathered a truck full of clothes and supplies and drove it to Iowa.

This rural Wisconsin village has a canning factory on each end of town. To handle the harvest, the community almost doubles in the summer. During those months a Spanish-speaking congregation gathers on Sunday afternoon. The town's ethanol plant has deeply divided residents and thus challenged the church to worship and serve as one body. Studies and worship focusing on healing and forgiveness offer opportunities for dialogue in the community.

In preparation for the 150th anniversary of First Presbyterian in Cambria the congregation decided to remodel the fellowship hall. Characteristically doing most of the work themselves, men and women, young and old, farmers and factory workers came together to pull down the ceiling and tear out the paneling and the flooring. Now they look forward to celebrating all year in the newly restored Heritage Hall.

The presbytery's 61 churches have 10,218 members. The University of Dubuque and University of Dubuque Theological Seminary are within its bounds.

Prayer

Savior God, what a privilege it is to be your hands and feet in this world. Give us eyes to see where we may come alongside and serve. Strengthen those engulfed by disaster. Empower us by your Spirit to freely minister in Jesus' name. Amen.

p2

Let us join in prayer for:

Presbytery Staff
Rev. Ken Meunier, executive presbyter
Judy Crotsenberg, presbytery administrator
Elder Alyson Janke, stated clerk

PC(USA) General Assembly Staff
Andrew Gamble, BOP
Rev. David Gambrell, GAMC

Daily Lectionary

☼ Ps. 92, 149 ☾ Ps. 23, 114
Exod. 13:17—14:4
2 Cor. 4:16—5:10; Mark 12:18–27

Sunday Lectionary and Hymns

Acts 5:27–32
The Strife Is O'er
PH 119, HB 203

Ps. 118:14–24
PH 231
Song of Zechariah
PH 602
or
Ps. 150
Praise Ye the Lord
PH 258

Rev. 1:4–8
All Hail the Power of Jesus' Name!
PH 142, 143, HB 132

John 20:19–31
O Sons and Daughters, Let Us Sing!
PH 116, 117, HB 206

Daily Lectionary
☼ Ps. 93, 150 ☾ Ps. 136, 117
Exod. 14:5–22
1 John 1:1–7; John 14:1–7

Holocaust Remembrance Day

The Lord's Day

Minute for Mission: Evangelical Seminary of Puerto Rico

In the Reformed tradition, theological formation is God's gift to those who, through the waters of baptism, take into themselves the identity of the Christian community. Acknowledging this gift, seminaries are required to consider the ways in which their resources and educational programs advance the formation of all those who seek the knowledge of Christ, whether they are following the vocation of ordained pastor or committed lay person.

As the Evangelical Seminary of Puerto Rico prepares to celebrate its ninety years of service to the church and God's people, it seeks to reinvigorate this theological responsibility. During the next three years, faculty and administrative staff will join faith communities throughout Puerto Rico to reflect on the themes of hope, joy, and freedom. Through a series of coordinated conferences and workshops at congregations, the seminary will gather regional clergy and lay leaders to engage in conversations about the future of the church that, it is hoped, will provide new frameworks for interpreting the church and its mission and, in turn, will make seminary education more in tune with the actual challenges and needs of living faith communities. To prepare dialogue partners for meaningful face-to-face conversations, a monthly reflection written by faculty members of El Seminario reaches pastors and congregations by electronic delivery once a week. Responses from pastors and lay people are welcomed as we build a community of learners not bounded by classroom time, degree requirements, and the physical boundaries of a seminary campus.

At the time we celebrate our one hundred years of ministry in 2019, we hope to proclaim faithfully that we have accompanied the church in the challenging task of forging God's realm.

—*Rev. Jose Irizarry, president, Evangelical Seminary of Puerto Rico*

Prayer
Gracious and loving God, give us humble hearts so that we can recognize the gifts of others and encourage the use of those gifts for the edification of your church and for the fulfillment of your mission. In the name of the One we call Teacher, Jesus Christ. Amen.

The Presbytery of Milwaukee

Wisconsin

Theologian Gustavo Gutierrez once said that doing theology is finding the gospel in any human situation. That is, even when we feel most challenged, God is already there.

Doing Christ's ministry within an immigrant community facing many social, political, and economic challenges wouldn't be possible without believing that Christ is already there. The great diversity of needs within the immigrant community has challenged Espíritu de Esperanza to be creative, recognize needs and limitations, and seek God's given gifts and tools for the work in the community.

Children visit the Angelic Organics farm.

The diverse needs and gifts have led Espíritu de Esperanza to become ecumenical, supported by Lutheran and Presbyterian churches, and to do ministry in relationship with many other organizations and denominations working with the Latino community.

Through this network the ministry provides bereavement support to Latino families who are unable to go back home to bury their dead; creates access to an organic farm, quality food, and a chance to love the land; advocates for immigrants rights' and better relationships with the local government; publishes a bimonthly Latino newspaper; broadcasts a weekly radio program called "Cristo Migrante"; and hosts the Mobile Mexican Consulate twice a year, which provides documents to hundreds of Mexican citizens who otherwise would have no way to prove their identity.

Since its beginning this ministry has provided for the gathering of an ecumenical worshiping community every Sunday, led by Lutheran and Presbyterian pastors.

The Presbytery of Milwaukee is proud to serve with 10,084 members in 46 congregations.

Prayer

Gracious God, allow us to find the way to your kingdom. Inspire us, challenge us, lead us, equip us. Fill us with your love and your joy as we grow in understanding and respond to your love for the world. Amen.

Let us join in prayer for:

Elder Janet Martin, member, GAMC

Presbytery Staff
Rev. P. Gregory Neel, executive presbyter
Elder Eileen Pierce, program coordinator
Elder Roxanne Lawrence, resource center coordinator
Rev. Willem Houts, stated clerk
Elder Detlef Pavlovich, treasurer
Elder Christine Halverson, administrative assistant

PC(USA) General Assembly Staff
Debbie Gardiner, GAMC
Ruth Gardner, GAMC
Elder Linda Garrett, GAMC

Daily Lectionary
☼ Ps. 97, 145 ☾ Ps. 124, 115
Exod. 14:21–31
1 Peter 1:1–12; John 14:(1–7) 8–17

The Presbytery of Minnesota Valleys

Members of Crosslake Presbyterian Church looked for ways to walk together in honoring Christ's love for one another. Tapping maple trees surfaced as a way for water (or maple sap, in this case) to flow out of the believer's heart. Then-pastor Ray Larson and members Dave Fischer and Don Hoger pooled their talents, time, and money for materials to tap 150 trees the first year. The church kept a few bottles to serve with a pancake breakfast, where proceeds were used to send youth to camp at Presbyterian Clearwater Forest, where the tapping occurs. The remaining cases were given to Clearwater to sell.

Juliet Holder and son Joshua from Plymouth Macalester Presbyterian learn to sap.

Four years later this "sapping" mission has grown to tapping four hundred trees and including volunteers from First Presbyterian Church, Brainerd, and Crosby Ironton Church, Crosby. Minnesota Department of Corrections "Sentence to Serve" misdemeanor inmates also help with this hard work. Some weekend confirmand groups and church retreat members are making sapping part of their fellowship and reflection time. The enthusiasm and camaraderie are contagious during collection of the sap.

CJ Amweg, a member of First Presbyterian, reflected that "something deeper took place in that wintry forest. One of the basic tenets of Christianity, the belief that more can be accomplished through cooperation to achieve a common goal, was put into practice. I was present for a very inspiring sermon, one preached through actions rather than words. It is not so much that the forest is like a cathedral, but if one takes the time to see rather than look, the forest becomes the cathedral."

The Presbytery of Minnesota Valleys has 65 churches and 9,297 members.

Prayer

Lord, let us not forget that in your infinite wisdom you created us to search for new ways to serve you. Awaken this desire to recognize these gifts, and give us the willingness to apply them. Amen.

The Presbytery of Missouri River Valley

Iowa, Nebraska

A Sudanese refugee family of nine arrived at an airfield in Omaha, Nebraska, in the bitter cold. After a 26-hour flight, they were hungry, the baby had only a scarf for a diaper, and the rest had only the clothes they wore. With two weeks' notice the church families of New Life Presbyterian and First Presbyterian churches in Omaha had prepared for the family's arrival. That night they were wrapped in winter clothes and welcomed in a church member's home. It was that night in the late 1990s that this mother, father, and children began their life in America.

The Rev. Goanar Chol of Des Moines, Iowa, asked if First Presbyterian could offer space in which Sudanese Presbyterians could worship in Omaha. The session said yes without hesitation. In 2000 the first twelve Sudanese united in membership, which has grown every year. In 2004 the Sudanese American Presbyterian Fellowship was established and moved into a church.

Michael Kuach, one of the first twelve members and the fellowship's commissioned lay pastor, asked First Church for use of the sanctuary for an interdenominational Christmas Day service. He promised it would be well attended by Sudanese from across Nebraska and Iowa and would last over two hours. The session again said yes.

On Christmas Day, with standing room only, children on parents' laps, and both balconies packed, First Presbyterian filled with voices shouting "Alleluia" and the sounds of drums and multiple choirs. Eight sermons and more than five hours later, a reported 2,002 Sudanese men, women, and children joyfully left the sanctuary. An exhausted Michael told First Presbyterian staff member Diane Plasek that he was sad that the celebration as a Christian community was over on that Christmas Day. So was Diane.

The Presbytery of Missouri River Valley works in partnership with 54 congregations serving 10,558 members.

Prayer

Lord, Quencher of our thirst, you are the living water flowing freely from the hearts of our Sudanese brothers and sisters. We praise you for the abundant evidence of your Spirit in their fellowship, and we ask your continued blessings upon the members of this faith community. We pray that all our faith communities might be filled with people whose hearts are overflowing with rivers of living water so that others might be drawn to you and know the joy of fellowship with and in you. Amen.

Let us join in prayer for:

Presbytery Staff
Rev. Kevin Keaton, executive presbyter
Rev. Steve Plank, stated clerk
Joan Royer, administrative assistant
Elder Geri Clanton, mission and mission interpretation committee chair

PC(USA) General Assembly Staff
Karen Geary, BOP
Elder Martha Gee, GAMC

Daily Lectionary
☼ Ps. 99, 147:1–11; ☾ Ps. 9, 118
Exod. 15:22—16:10
1 Peter 2:1–10; John 15:1–11

Let us join in prayer for:

Presbytery Staff
Rev. David A. Feltman, general presbyter
Blake Wood, stated clerk
Lee Nicholas, treasurer
Kaylene Hoskins, administrative assistant
Vicki Thordsen, secretary

PC(USA) General Assembly Staff
Rev. Philip Gehman, BOP
David Geiger, OGA
Nicole Gerkins, GAMC

The Presbytery of North Central Iowa

The chapel fills quickly. People greet each other in Spanish before the service begins. Five different countries are represented in this animated group. The pastor greets everyone heartily. Prayer begins to flow from the pastor and others in the room. The singing is joyful and lively—even the children join in. The powerful words of the pastor generate enthusiastic responses. The sharing of peace is in the heartfelt greeting of each person. Even a non-Spanish speaker know the presence of the Spirit.

The Fort Dodge Hispanic ministry enjoys music before worship.

This Hispanic ministry in Fort Dodge, Iowa, was begun through a Special Ministries matching grant in 2004 and has been supported by the Presbytery of North Central Iowa for the past two years. The congregation had grown to almost fifty men, women, and children in 2009. It is led by the Rev. Bienvenido Acosta from the Dominican Republic and serves Spanish-speaking people within a 45-mile radius of Fort Dodge. In addition to evangelism and worship, he teaches several Bible studies in the area, facilitates fellowship, and provides social support to the Hispanic/Latino population. The ministry is a source of hope for many who struggle, and it provides a church family for all who come to worship Christ. A new vision for the congregation is to strive to become a new church development within the next five years and the presbytery's first since the 1960s.

The Presbytery of North Central Iowa has 8,806 members in 54 churches.

Daily Lectionary
☼ Ps. 47, 147:12–20 ☾ Ps. 68, 113
Exod. 16:10–22
1 Peter 2:11—3:12; John 15:12–27

Prayer
Lord God, you surprise us continually with your presence, which is always at work to gather your people. We are humbled by your grace as we see this ministry growing into a Hispanic Presbyterian congregation. Give us the wisdom, imagination, and love to support them so that ultimately Jesus Christ will receive the glory of their praise. Amen.

The Presbytery of Northern Plains

North Dakota, Minnesota, Montana

For over a decade, the Presbytery of the Northern Plains (PNP) has been exploring what it means to be the church in partnership with the Chogoria North, Central, and South presbyteries of the Presbyterian Church of East Africa. The partnership has participated in traditional mission activities involving visits, fundraising, and building projects—but the vision that has developed among the people from both sides has a different focus. The partnership seeks to build a relationship as brothers and sisters in Christ by expanding the participants' knowledge of what it means in another land to be a Presbyterian and increasing understanding of lifestyles in a culture that differs from their own; praying for one another, sharing one another's joys and sorrows and needs, and lifting one another up before God; networking through sister congregations, which will enable friendship and sharing on a more personal level; and supporting one another in their spiritual, social, and program needs.

PNP visitors pose with friends from partner churches in Kajiampau, Tharaka, Kenya, in the summer of 2008.

The evidence of God's blessings on the partnership is not seen primarily in buildings constructed, scholarships raised, or supplies donated, but in the regular exchange of letters and e-mails between friends in Kenya and the Northern Plains. They are also evident in the weekly prayers offered by churches for their sister congregations in their joint Bible study, and in the growing recognition that all are truly members of one body.

The Presbytery of the Northern Plains includes Jamestown College and 1 Korean fellowship and has 6,473 members in 64 churches.

Prayer

O Lord, our God, we praise you for calling people for yourself from among all nations. Grant that by the work of the Holy Spirit, we might come to closer unity with our brothers and sisters around the world. In Jesus' name. Amen.

Let us join in prayer for:

Presbytery Staff
Steve Minnema, interim executive presbyter
Michael Lochow, stated clerk
Bill Cawley, treasurer
Laurie Elhard, communication coordinator

PC(USA) General Assembly Staff
Lacey Gilliam, GAMC
Sharon Gillies, GAMC

Daily Lectionary

☼ Ps. 96, 148 ☾ Ps. 49, 138
Exod. 16:23–36
1 Peter 3:13—4:6; John 16:1–15

The Presbytery of Northern Waters

Minnesota, Wisconsin, Michigan

Presbyterian Clearwater Forest (PCF) is a beautiful camp and conference center located in the Brainerd Lakes region of central Minnesota. Its ownership is shared among the presbyteries of Minnesota Valleys, Northern Plains, Northern Waters, Twin Cities Area, and the Synod of Lakes and Prairies. Since 1954 Presbyterians have gathered at this site that now encompasses 1,017 acres and has 3½ miles of undeveloped shoreline. Pristine Clearwater Lake is known for its water quality and is the headwaters of the Nokasippi River, a short tributary of the Mississippi River. Working through year-round volunteers and seasonal staff, and utilizing both historic and modern facilities, the Holy Spirit continues to flow through dynamic retreats, conferences, and summer camp experiences.

Eagle Lodge, constructed in 1922, is part of the Clearwater Forest Conference Center.

The Presbytery of Northern Waters provides annual camping scholarships to its youth, and it supports the biennial Clearwater Conference featuring worship, keynote speakers, and workshops for study and reflection. Each May Clearwater Cleanup Days are held to prepare the summer camp facilities for a season of outreach to more than 800 campers. These work days include everything from picking up sticks and cleaning windows to major renovations that enhance safety and help adjust to the camp's growth. Presbyterian Women hold their Women's Retreat at PCF every three years. Some of the churches within the presbytery host Camp Sundays that celebrate PCF as an extension of the ministry and mission of their congregations.

The Presbytery of Northern Waters has 60 churches with 6,978 members.

Prayer

Gracious God, we rejoice in the many ways you are present with this presbytery as we share a beautiful place set apart for the important ministry of Jesus Christ. We thank you that people from near and far come and experience Christian community, hospitality, and the inspiration of your Spirit. Continue to guide the staff and volunteers in your work. Amen.

Daily Lectionary
☼ Ps. 92, 149 ☾ Ps. 23, 114
Exod. 17:1–16
1 Peter 4:7–19; John 16:16–33

The Lord's Day

Minute for Mission: Health Awareness

A 2009 poll conducted by the PC(USA)'s former office of National Health Ministries found that concern about health care cost and availability outranks worry about the environment, crime, war, and the economic downturn. Two-thirds of the respondents had, in the previous year, experienced cost increases in insurance or limitations in or loss of health care coverage.

One of the most frequently cited issues among older respondents is apprehension that they will outlive their savings and, even if they have insurance, will be unable to pay their portion of medical costs. Many shared their individual stories. Some had been denied access to health care insurance because of preexisting conditions. Some had lost health insurance because of unaffordable premiums or job loss. Others wrote of medical debt that resulted in bankruptcy, second mortgages, sale of personal possessions, delayed retirement, and myriad life changes. A final group of respondents were older adults with adult children who have a disability requiring them to live in an assisted or supervised setting. These stories were particularly wrenching as people wrote of their fears that cherished adult children might end up on the streets or in crowded institutions after their parents died.

These stories were for the most part shared by people who have had access to care and the benefits of information about wellness and prevention. In the United States, 47 million people are without any access to care, and their numbers increase daily.

During the past three decades, the Presbyterian General Assembly has repeatedly called upon the federal government and our elected officials to find a way to provide universal basic health care. It is important that all of us advocate for expanded basic health care. Working for this social justice has never been more critical than it is today.

—*Pat Gleich, former associate, National Health Ministries,*
General Assembly Mission Council

Prayer

Caring Creator who promised abundant life for all of your children, shape our words and actions to effectively address the inequities and disparities in health care. Strengthen our resolve to be leaders as we speak for those who sit outside both the health care system and the circles where decisions about health care are made. In the name of Christ. Amen.

Sunday, April 18

Sunday Lectionary and Hymns

Acts 9:1–6 (7–20)
Make Me a Captive, Lord
PH 378, HB 308

Ps. 30
Come Sing to God
PH 181
O Lord, by Thee Delivered
HB 127

Rev. 5:11–14
Blessing and Honor
PH 147, HB 137

John 21:1–19
Hope of the World
PH 360, HB 291

Daily Lectionary

☼ Ps. 93, 150 ☾ Ps. 136, 117
Exod. 18:1–12
1 John 2:7–17; Mark 16:9–20

The Presbytery of Prospect Hill

Iowa, Nebraska

When the members of the mission team of First Presbyterian Church in Sioux City, Iowa, went to Haiti in March 2008, they looked for the best location to build a water treatment system. The entire group agreed on Trinity House in Jacmel. Their decision was confirmed by the story of Ritchy, one of the students served by Trinity House's ministries. Ritchy and his siblings' home was seriously damaged by Hurricane Gustav. Mudslides and severe flooding washed away many of the family's possessions, and high winds blew off their roof. They also lost their chickens and a goat.

School children at Trinity House will be served by the new clean water system in Jacmel, Haiti.

Although Haiti can receive an abundance of water, sometimes this water causes serious damage to the property and possessions of families who are already struggling. What's more, it does not necessarily provide the clean water that the village of Jacmel and others like it so desperately need.

The Presbytery of Prospect Hill is partnering with Living Waters for the World and Trinity House to install a clean water system that will provide Trinity House, its school, and the families it serves in Jacmel with a steady supply of clean water for many years to come.

The Living Waters Working Group is one of the first two working groups formed under the new Mission Design that the presbytery adopted in 2008. The presbytery continues to seek God's mission for churches in its own communities and beyond.

The presbytery includes Buena Vista University, the Presbyterian Camp on Lake Okojobi, and 57 churches with 8,330 members.

Prayer
Dear Lord, we thank you for allowing us the privilege of serving your kingdom. Guide our steps as we reach out to share the good news of the gospel with our neighbors both near and far. In Jesus' name we pray. Amen.

The Presbytery of South Dakota

It is more than a mission project of Olive Presbyterian Church in Platte, South Dakota. It's about relationships of believers—relationships between neighbors, generations, and cultures that span denominations and state lines.

Because many residents of Wanblee heat their homes solely by wood, each month a huge truckload of wood is collected, chopped, and delivered by the residents of Platte.

Members of the congregation of all ages have joined forces with the seven other churches in Platte, a town of about 1,350 people, to extend helping hands and loving hearts to the residents of Wanblee, South Dakota. Wanblee is on the Pine Ridge Indian Reservation about 150 miles west of Platte, and its residents, largely members of the Oglala Sioux tribe, are among the poorest people in the nation.

Every month a group of volunteers from Platte goes to Wanblee. They bring the basics—firewood, blankets, and food. While they're there they engage in friendly chats and even such services as cutting hair and painting fingernails. The activities are coordinated through the All Nations Assembly of God in Mission. They've constructed a building addition and sorted and distributed donated clothing and toys. Candles for donation were collected by the Presbytery of South Dakota, with its 69 churches and 8,253 members. Congregations in other states have expressed an interest in participating in this mission in Wanblee.

The visits offer the continuing opportunity to talk and worship together. Hundreds of people from Platte and Wanblee are experiencing firsthand the grace of God as these communities, with their different cultures, become more than just neighbors. Through relational evangelism the parties show and are shown Christ's love through actions and the message that "God loves you."

Prayer

Creator God, you have blessed the world with spiritual diversity. We pray that the Holy Spirit and the Power of the East of the Lakota people will, as we worship together, grant each of us the wisdom that perfects and unites what has been already given to us by you. Amen.

Tuesday, April 20

Let us join in prayer for:

Presbytery Staff
Meleta DeJong, moderator
Evelyn Reynen, stated clerk
Hal Neller, administrator
Wendy Monson, administrative assistant

PC(USA) General Assembly Staff
Nancy Goodhue, GAMC
Theresa Goodlin, GAMC

Daily Lectionary
☼ Ps. 98, 146 ☾ Ps. 66, 116
Exod. 19:1–16
Col. 1:1–14; Matt. 3:7–12

The Presbytery of the Twin Cities Area

Minnesota, Wisconsin

Children were playing in the parking lot of Arlington Hills Presbyterian Church on the east side of St. Paul, Minnesota. The Christian educator, Sally Narr, began conversations of welcome—those first steps of evangelism. "Hola! Cómo esta usted? Yes, you can play here."

Soon children rang the church doorbell. "I'm thirsty. Do you have water?" Of course! God's people not only offer water in a cup, but the living water through Jesus Christ. The doorbell became urgent. "I'm hungry. Do you have something to eat?" Of course! God's people provided nutritious snacks, introducing the Bread of Life through Jesus Christ. The children were persistent. "Does the church have something fun for us to do?" Of course! God's people gave them watercolors. The children started coming to Sunday school. However, they wanted much more, and the Christian Education Committee felt God calling it to provide more. Creative energy began to rush like rivers of living water. Seed money was donated by the presbytery, and funds came from the PC(USA). Local foundations made endowments. The Eastside Children's Summer Program was born.

Teen volunteers Charlie and Cece help add details within the Amazon rainforest mural designed by children.

The eight-week program begins each day with lunch. The children are taught science concepts, art techniques, and healthy self-esteem. They are helped with literacy activities. The program is a Youth Job Corps site for teens in the St. Paul area.

The program provides a ministry of presence so children learn that Jesus Christ is revealed through God's people, who act in love. The Presbytery of the Twin Cities Area's 69 churches have 25,358 members.

Prayer

O God, Creator of children: we offer to you believers' hearts. May we boldly present the gospel with arms wide open to children in our midst—thirsting for the Living Water and the Bread of Life. Energize us with creativity and imagination so that our acts of love become acts of hope. Amen.

Earth Day

Minute for Mission

Last year on Earth Day at Stone Church of Willow Glen in San Jose, California, pastor Ken Henry dressed as nineteenth-century naturalist John Muir and preached about reverence for the earth and our common responsibility. But at this PC(USA) church, every day is Earth Day.

Stone Church members hike at Rancho Canada del Oro Open Space Preserve.

Congregational activities such as Bike to Church Sunday, hikes for all ages on Earth Appreciation Day, and Green Sunday with "green men" leading the children's sermon have encouraged members to increase their commitment to care for God's earth. The garden volunteers suggested replacing a church lawn with drought-tolerant plants, and planting them became a youth member's Eagle Scout project. One teen initiated an Earth Friends summer church school series, and recently church members created a Cool Cuisine Luncheon to highlight the environmental benefits of eating locally grown organic products. Stone Church was honored to become certified as a green business in Santa Clara County due to its low energy and water use practices.

Lately Stone Church has partnered with Acterra, an environmental nonprofit, to offer the Cool Campaign to church members and friends. This program provides a lifestyle focus each month, with suggested actions and new habits that members can adopt at home, school, or work. By acting on challenges, members have prevented significant carbon dioxide emissions. Coffee-hour conversations include bragging about low electric bills and the pleasures of sleeping on line-dried sheets. The campaign helps heighten members' awareness and gives concrete ways to practice a better lifestyle of going green in deep, sustained, and meaningful ways.

—*Rhonda Lakatos, member, Stone Church of Willow Glen, San Jose, California*

Prayer

God who created the heavens and the earth, thank you for the witness of congregations such as Stone Church of Willow Glen. May their model of creation care and personal lifestyle integrity inspire us to make every day your Earth Day. In Jesus' name. Amen.

Thursday, April 22

Let us join in prayer for:

PC(USA) General Assembly Staff
Catherine Gordon, GAMC
Dorothea Gordon, BOP
Lewis Gordon, BOP

Daily Lectionary
☼ Ps. 47, 147:12–20 ☾ Ps. 68, 113
Exod. 20:1–21
Col. 1:24—2:7; Matt. 4:1–11

Let us join in prayer for:

Presbytery Staff
Rev. Dr. Lucille K. Rupe,
executive presbyter
Rev. Sarah Moore-Nokes, associate
executive presbyter
Rev. Dr. Michael B. Lukens, stated clerk
Elder Nancy Barczak, associate
for administration

PC(USA) General Assembly Staff
Denise Govindarajan, GAMC
Angela Gowdy, GAMC

The Presbytery of Winnebago

Wisconsin

Just Fare Market seeks to be a Kingdom on Earth builder so that poor and disadvantaged people will not be thirsty for lack of drinking water and will experience the hope and eternal thirst quenching of Jesus Christ.

Members of First Presbyterian Church, Fond du Lac, who sponsored SERRV sales asked the church in 2004 to commit to using fair trade coffee. In November 2006 these members stepped out in faith to set up a trial fair trade shop. After an encouraging Christmas season, the session granted permission to continue, Just Fare Market was registered as a nonstock corporation, and ecumenical partners were secured.

Just Fare's development involves trust and waiting in "holy tension" as God provides people skills and resources. Its primary mission is education about the benefits of fair trade and reflection on the impact of consumption on social justice and environmental sustainability.

Linda Neville admires a recycled paper platter made by artisans in Vietnam.

Just Fare (www.justfare.org) is a retail link in the alternative trading chain, partnering with long-standing organizations such as SERRV and newer groups such as Partners for Just Trade, Import Peace, and Nueva Vida. The market offers fair trade coffee, tea, and chocolate as well as handcrafts for gift giving or personal use. The artisans and farmers who supply Just Fare Market are empowered with hope and love to build their businesses and develop quality sustainable products.

The Presbytery of Winnebago serves 40 congregations with 7,795 members.

Prayer

Let my heart be broken . . . with the things that break the heart of God, and let my feet be led to places he has trod. Let my hands be clenched in that place of prayer that I may reach his heart so others may find life in there. Amen.

Prayer by Bob Pierce and Ellen Willis (Togetherwecandosomething.com)

Daily Lectionary
☼ Ps. 96, 148 ☾ Ps. 49, 138
Exod. 24:1–18
Col. 2:8–23; Matt. 4:12–17

Asia and the Pacific

Mongolia
North Korea
South Korea
China
Japan
Bhutan
Nepal
Burma
Taiwan
Pakistan
India
Laos
Bangladesh
Cambodia
Thailand
Vietnam
Philippines
Sri Lanka
Brunei
Maldives
Malaysia
Micronesia
Palau
Singapore
Papua New Guinea
Nauru
Indonesia
Solomon Islands
East Timor
Tuvalu
Kiribati
Vanuatu
Samoa
Fiji
Australia
Tonga
New Zealand
Marshall Islands

Prayer

Merciful God, open our eyes to see Christ in the struggles and ministries of sisters and brothers in Asia, where your Spirit is on the move to transform creation. Move us to weep with those who weep, serve where we are able, and celebrate the work of the Holy Spirit to bring justice for all. May the grace of Christ guide our relationships in Asia and the Pacific, that God's kingdom may be realized on earth as it is in heaven. Amen.

Saturday, April 24

Let us join in prayer for:

PC(USA) People in Mission
David Walter, mission volunteer, regional partnership facilitator, World Mission

PC(USA) General Assembly Staff
Helena Grabowski, GAMC
Roberta Grant, BOP
Teresa Grant, GAMC

Daily Lectionary

☼ Ps. 92, 149 ☾ Ps. 23, 114
Exod. 25:1–22
Col. 3:1–17; Matt. 4:18–25

Sunday Lectionary and Hymns

Acts 9:36–43
I Sing a Song of the Saints of God
PH 364

Ps. 23
The Lord's My Shepherd, I'll Not Want
PH 170, HB 104

Rev. 7:9–17
Ye Servants of God, Your Master Proclaim
PH 477, HB 27

John 10:22–30
Savior, Like a Shepherd Lead Us
PH 387, HB 380

Daily Lectionary

✹ Ps. 93, 150 ☾ Ps. 136, 117
Exod. 28:1–4, 30–38
1 John 2:18–29; Mark 6:30–44

The Lord's Day

Minute for Mission: Rural Life Ministry

What started in 2002 as a question—"Do you suppose seminarians would travel to rural North Dakota to study and become acquainted with rural ministry?"—has become a week-long, annual event called Seminary on the Prairie. It is sponsored by Luther Seminary in St. Paul, Minnesota, and the eight Evangelical Lutheran Church of America congregations and one PC(USA) congregation in eastern North Dakota (First Presbyterian of Cooperstown) that make up Tri-County Ministry. Since 2006, the event has been held at Red Willow Bible Camp in rural Binford, North Dakota. Students from Luther Seminary have been attending Seminary on the Prairie for the last several years.

From the inception of Seminary on the Prairie, Tri-County Ministry's desire has been to introduce seminarians to rural ministry in North Dakota. To aid interaction between Tri-County members and seminarians, housing for seminarians has been offered in the homes of Tri-County members. Many of the host families still communicate with past seminarians who stayed in their homes and are now pastors. The seminary doesn't just engage seminarians: from the beginning it has also offered rural educational topics that often interest church members, lay leaders, and pastors in an educational setting in eastern North Dakota.

The future of Seminary on the Prairie as a rural educational offering is so important to Tri-County Ministry that in 2009 its council approved a line item amount for the seminary. In addition, Tri-County has a new planning committee for the seminary consisting of interested church members. In January, the topic for the event was "Cooperative Ministries." The focus for 2011 will be on geriatric ministry. More information is available at www.tricountyministry.org.

—*Rev. Marli Danielson, co-pastor, First Presbyterian Church,*
Cooperstown, North Dakota

Prayer

O Lord, we thank you for the opportunity to help new leaders become familiar with rural settings. We ask that you guide all involved in planning and carrying out this ministry and continue to use it for the glory of your kingdom. In your Son's name we pray. Amen.

Asia and the Pacific, *continued*

Let us join in prayer for:

PC(USA) General Assembly Staff
Angel Green, BOP
Joanne Green, OGA

As the center of Christianity shifts to the global south, this may be the century of Asia. An apt description of what is happening in Asia is "the rise of the rest"—the ascendency of giants like China and India. Unfortunately too many have been left on the sidelines, particularly those in minority faith communities, some of whom are our longest standing mission partners.

With almost two thirds of the world's inhabitants, this region is experiencing such challenges as regional wars, economic injustice, natural disasters, poverty, hunger, militarization, human rights abuses, internal displacement, corruption, pollution, and religious persecution. Amid these conditions we give thanks for God's presence! Asian faith communities offer tangible words of hope and visible signs of the Spirit.

Post-Olympic China has shown the world what it can do. Now it must address how progress can be sustained without violating the sanctity of life and the rights of its 1.4 billion people. Churches continue to attract worshipers, and growth is evident in certain regions. China's post-denominational expression of faith is young, and it challenges the global church to overcome our particularities that separate and divide.

The Presbyterian Church of Taiwan is using new forms of media to reach out. Our longstanding partner, the Presbyterian Church of Korea, forges ahead with a campaign to add 300,000 members to reach the 3 million mark! The church in Korea shows spiritual vitality, financial strength, and a mission-sending capacity that reaches the far corners of the globe.

While Sri Lanka, Nepal, Myanmar, Bangladesh, Thailand, and the Philippines experience political unrest and internal power struggles, we affirm our solidarity with the churches and institutions in these contexts.

Indonesia, which has the largest Muslim population in the world, has a moderate approach to respecting peoples' differences with tolerance. The churches have entered into the dialogue to support this hopeful middle way.

Prayer

Eye-opening God, help your church to catch a glimpse of your Spirit's work in Asia, where the gospel is rooted and your church is alive. Enable us to learn from others who have a different way of seeing, knowing, and living. May the witness of your people in Asia and the Pacific, through their churches and ministries, stir our hearts, prick our consciences, and change our lives for the good of your world. In Jesus' name. Amen.

Daily Lectionary

☼ Ps. 97, 145 ☾ Ps. 124, 115
Exod. 32:1–20
Col. 3:18—4:6 (7–18); Matt. 5:1–10

Asia and the Pacific, *continued*

Pakistan gropes to find a way to move ahead as violence escalates and a peaceful transition toward political stability remains elusive. Our church partner offers hope that the way ahead will come through books, not bullets or bombs.

Within India this past year violent attacks on the Christian community in Orissa and Karnataka shocked the world. Our partner, the Church of North India, which covers two thirds of the country, lives out a strong witness to the good news and is growing. It labors to bring congregational renewal so that churches can effectively engage in mission at the local level.

Leaders of the Church of North India participate in renewal training in Nagpur.

The global church must "groan and sigh" as the Pacific region islands endure the consequences from global warming, even though the islands' inhabitants themselves create no significant carbon footprint.

Give thanks for mission co-workers who walk alongside brothers and sisters doing justice, evangelizing, educating, providing health and wholeness, and working for peace as they bear witness to the transforming power of the gospel. Thanks be to God for the witness and sacrifices of Asian brothers and sisters from whom we have much to learn.

As you read their stories in the following pages, pray and continue to support the vital witness of the church in this vast and varied region.

–*Rev. David L. Hudson, area coordinator, Asia and the Pacific,
General Assembly Mission Council*

Daily Lectionary
☼ Ps. 98, 146 ☾ Ps. 66, 116
Exod. 32:21–34
1 Thess. 1:1–10; Matt. 5:11–16

Prayer
God of justice and mercy, open us to Asian hospitality, which models vulnerability, self-sacrifice, and mutuality, qualities often in short supply in our culture. May we hear the prophetic witness of the two-thirds world to live simply so that others may simply live. In Jesus' name. Amen.